About the Author

I have been writing engineering technical books for some forty years now. In such types of books, one is not permitted to include emotional words. I told myself that it is high time I started letting my emotions run wild through the writing of satirical-type publications.

Please, Just Call Me Kevie!

Lord Christopher

Please, Just Call Me Kevie!

Olympia Publishers
London

www.olympiapublishers.com
OLYMPIA PAPERBACK EDITION

Copyright © Lord Christopher 2022

The right of Lord Christopher to be identified as author of
this work has been asserted in accordance with sections 77 and 78
of the Copyright, Designs and Patents Act 1988.

All Rights Reserved

No reproduction, copy or transmission of this publication
may be made without written permission.
No paragraph of this publication may be reproduced,
copied or transmitted save with the written permission of the
publisher, or in accordance with the provisions
of the Copyright Act 1956 (as amended).

Any person who commits any unauthorised act in relation to
this publication may be liable to criminal
prosecution and civil claims for damage.

A CIP catalogue record for this title is
available from the British Library.

ISBN: 978-1-80074-473-8

This is a work of creative nonfiction. The events are portrayed to the
best of the author's memory. While all the stories in this book are
true, some names and identifying details have been changed to
protect the privacy of the people involved.

First Published in 2022

Olympia Publishers
Tallis House
2 Tallis Street
London
EC4Y 0AB

Printed in Great Britain

Dedication

I dedicate this book to my better half, my beautiful wife, Anne, who has battled, and is still battling Parkinson's Disease and has recently survived the awful breast cancer journey.

Acknowledgements

A big thank you to my paternal Uncle Kevin who has lived a life full of challenges and adventure, a small part of which is presented in this book.

Chapter 1
Friday night dreams

It was late summer. The early afternoon was unusually humid. A picturesque sky gave way to a series of clouds roaming high overhead, just like Brown's cows, coming in from the south. The air was very still. The atmosphere was close. Rain had not fallen for many weeks, which is unusual for this 'down under' part of the world at this time of year. The oppressiveness was all around. If you raised your arm your armpits would immediately sweat.

My wife Anne and I were sitting on our newly constructed upper front verandah, enjoying several cool drinks and a lively chat about nothing in particular. We enjoyed this new outdoor space because it was fresh and comfortable. We habitually frequented this space at every opportunity. It is secluded from our street.

Our serenity was interrupted by the arrival of a white panel van that stopped in front of our house. It parked itself under our golden melaleuca tree, most probably to seek shade away from the sun. There was no movement inside this curious van for what seemed like several minutes. No soul immediately alighted, so we knew it was not under the control of a courier driver, nor a real estate agent, or similar. In soft whispers between us, we wondered if the driver understood where he or she was, or where he or she was going.

"Maybe it's Uber Eats?" Anne whispered so softly that I only just caught her words.

"Could be, but I haven't ordered in," I responded.

During our whispered interlude, our telephone rang. I briskly jumped up from my seat (well, as best I could for my age) and so proceeded to the beckoning telephone, but by the time I had arrived in the living room, it had stopped.

I returned to my wife. "Any movement yet?"

"None whatsoever—I wonder who it is." My wife was still watching the white panel van very intently.

"Maybe whoever they might be are visiting the new people across the street," I suggested.

An event such as this in our younger years could easily have presented some sort of opportunity for us, but now, in our twilight years, it usually presented trouble.

A cool breeze rolled in from the east, as the sun, covered over by the clouds, briefly reappeared again, and cast some light inside the van. We could make out a silhouette at the wheel, but could not discern whether the silhouette was male, female, or indeed human. Several more minutes passed before we saw a slight movement. As we peered intently, we heard a *clunk*, followed by the driver's side door slowly opening, followed by a subsequent squeal. We could then make out the body parts of an elderly man.

He alighted with a haphazard movement away from our peering position. We could see his back. We could also make out a shock of collar-length white hair. He stalled, and then took several steps away from us, so we started to think he was visiting the new neighbours across the street. Suddenly, he turned sideways, and then turned again, so his final manoeuvre caused him to face our house. His white hair resembled the white clouds above. We still had some difficulty making out any other defining features. He stood there for what seemed like several more minutes.

The clouds then quickly gave way to sunshine, which accentuated the elderly man's chiselled features. We could see him looking over to our house as if staking it out. He then gazed at his phone. He proceeded to move towards our front gate. We easily understood from his movement that he had a disability. He was assisting his awkward walking with a stick, and, as he moved towards us, he exhibited a jerky gait that made me feel for him.

"Finally I can see someone—but who is it?" Anne enquired of me.

"Don't know, my darling," I responded uncertainly, but something in my subconscious was telling me, *you know this man—he is familiar!* The stranger continued his uncoordinated approach, negotiating the kerb, ducking under a low branch of the golden melaleuca tree, and then moved across the uneven footpath to finally reach our front gate.

As he approached, I stood up to get a closer, more detailed look. Upon seeing my movement, the stranger, who was about to dial his phone once he reached our gate, looked up, and then called out to us in a booming voice, which I'm sure all our neighbours heard: "Hi, Chris and Anne! It's Kevie here! I tried to ring youse to let youse know I was comin'! No answer!"

I returned in the same booming fashion, "Hi there, Kevin. Stay there, I'm coming down."

I excitedly descended the internal front stairs and proceeded to open the front door to find my paternal uncle Kevin standing there with a big grin on his face. I opened the security screen door and extended my right hand to shake his, and then said, "Hello Uncle Kevin, what a surprise! What are you doing here?"

Kevin tilted the left side of his head towards me, looked at me with his wide-open left eye (a bit like Rooster Cogburn in *True Grit*—except Rooster only had one eye). He then exclaimed, "Call me Kevie—everyone calls me Kevie!"

I have always had a problem addressing my uncle as 'Kevie'. My view of the world is that this diminishes respect for the elder. Indeed, I think most people today have lost respect for each other. No longer do you hear 'Mr' or 'Mrs' being used in salutation—except where it has morphed into 'Mr K' or 'Mrs O' at times. My mother always reminded me to be respectful of everyone, "including yourself". Maybe this is the single most problem we now have in this fast-paced, modern world—a general lack of respect for each other.

I was a little taken aback by Kevin's request, but responded with, "No worries, *Kevie*. Come up and join us for a beer!"

Both of his eyes widened with pleasant surprise, and he then said, "Beauty! Sounds good."

In a split second, I realised Kevin might not be able to use our stairs to access our upper level. It must have been the look on my face when I glanced from his skinny legs to the internal stairs that gave me away.

Reading my face, he offered, "I can take the stairs, no worries. I always like to challenge meself."

I went up first and stood waiting at the top of the stairs for him. He awkwardly moved himself up, one leg and one stair at a time, ably assisted by his walking stick. Once he reached the upper level, we both moved to the upper front verandah to join Anne, who was still looking perplexed and focusing intently on the white panel van.

Kevin moved over to Anne, bent down (with some noticeable difficulty), and declared, "Hello, Anne. Gee your lookin' good!"

A flustered Anne responded with, "Hi, Kevin. What are you doing here?"

Kevin's enthusiastic smile spread right across his face as he pleaded, "Please! Just call me Kevie—everyone calls me Kevie!" Then he added, "I see ya have ya Parkys well under control. How long's it bin?"

Like me, Anne's breath was taken away by Kevin's zeal, but she quickly composed herself and responded. "It was around Mother's Day several years ago that I was diagnosed."

I thought this might be an appropriate time to enquire into his disability, so I awkwardly blurted out, "Looks like you're still getting around OK, Kevie. Your legs are still serving you well?"

Kevin looked down at his skinny legs, then returned my gaze and said, "Mota-new-ron. Like Anne, it's under control. My doctor quietly recommended I take hoochie-cooch on a daily basis."

Upon hearing this, Anne became very uneasy. Just to explain; Anne does not partake of "hoochie-cooch". She daily ingests a dopamine drug through the course of the day to keep her Parkinson's disease under control. The only problem she has is dealing with a lack of balance and melancholy moods from time to time.

"What's hoochie-cooch?" I enquired, acting naive, "and what do you mean 'quietly'?"

"You know—grass, shit—marijuana!" replied Kevin. "And quietly, because doctors aren't allowed to prescribe the stuff," he whispered.

Kevin informed us that, when he was first diagnosed with motor neuron disease, his world fell apart. As most people know, motor neuron disease shortens one's life expectancy. Kevin felt his passion for driving and meeting people would be taken away. I remember Kevin always as a driver. He could never stay still as a passenger. He would drive anywhere and everywhere, and it didn't matter how far the distance. When he was younger, his driving on public roads was often described as *racy*. His fetish was tailgating. MND put a stop to that behaviour.

At one time in his life, Kevin was a racing car driver. He raced a 'brick' (Morris Mini-Minor) around Heddon Greta Speedway. I would often visit him in his home workshop to seek out advice on such issues as how to repair the sedan that I had crashed several times. Kevin possessed many practical methods about how to repair a motor vehicle. "With a packet'a band-aids, duct tape an' rubber bands," he would often say back then.

Kevin proceeded to tell us that his specialist doctor recommended he regularly partake of marijuana, at least one joint a day. My uncle explained that his medical specialist had conducted research into the beneficial use of marijuana for controlling motor neuron symptoms and delaying the progression of the disease. This medical specialist referenced

Kevin as his case study, given that Kevin was exhibiting a good quality of life over a prolonged period. Apparently, the medical research paper was never published because of the anti-marijuana lobby.

"Have a seat," I offered, pointing to the guest chair on our new verandah.

Kevin uncomfortably sat down on his appointed chair and then noticed that lying under it, was our dog Snoopy. Looking at Anne, he exclaimed, "Who's this?"

Snoopy opened his eyes, took one look at Kevin, groaned, flopped back onto his side, and then went quickly back to sleep. Kevin added, "I feel sorry for people who don't have a dog—they have to pick up the food scraps they drop!" The look of affection on my uncle's face as he stroked Snoopy told me these two were going to have a great friendship.

At the time of Kevin's arrival, Elle and Snoopy were our two pet dogs. Elle, a Staffordshire bull terrier, was out back. She was going deaf due to her age, so she probably didn't hear Kevin arrive. Elle was always very loyal and protective. She was only six months old when she stepped in to protect me from being attacked by a much larger dog as we walked in our neighbourhood. Elle jumped in and grabbed the mongrel around its throat as it lunged at me. The mongrel yelped and then ran away. It stopped about 20 metres away, still yelping, and then decided it would be brave, so turned it around and came running back at us. In true Staffie style, Elle lowered her back legs and waited. As the mongrel came within a metre of us, she lunged and grabbed the mongrel by the throat once more. The mongrel yelped again and took off, never to be seen again.

Elle had been through many bouts with skin cancer and managed to survive. She was a very active dog. She loved to go on her daily walk to the local park and chase water dragons into the creek. There were three billabongs through which she loved to skip. Of our animal menagerie, my favourite was Elle.

Snoopy, our ten-year-old Welsh cardigan corgi, didn't care who Kevin was, he just wanted to sleep. Kevin continued to introduce himself to Snoopy through touch as our big boy lay sleeping. "How many animals do youse have?" he asked.

We presented to Kevin a history of our animal menagerie. Anne was a daycare mother for twenty-five years. She dutifully cared for other people's children in our house, as well as skilfully raising our two sons. Anne firmly believed in providing a friendly family environment for all children in her care. She had a big capacity for love of other people's children, as well as our own. At that time, she was the *Mary Poppins* of our neighbourhood.

To provide a normal family home environment, we had assembled two dogs, two cats, twelve guinea pigs, six budgerigars, six Bourke's parrots and six chickens. It was the custom for the children in care to look after this animal menagerie; to collect the chicken eggs in the morning, and to feed all the animals daily. These chores gave each of the children a sense of belonging, which, in turn, nurtured learning and responsibility. I am very sure each child carried this sense of belonging, learning and responsibility into their adulthood.

From time to time, several of the former children in care, now grown up, have approached Anne in the street, or a shop, or when we have been dining out, to say, "Hello, remember me?" and, "Thank you". I think that those unsolicited friendly approaches are testament to her high quality of care and love.

Looking back, I don't know how, when or where Anne found time to rest. Back in those days, Anne was a very independent, strong and assertive woman. I labelled her the *little red hen* because, when she would ask someone to do something for her, she would ask only once, not twice, and when it was not done, she would do it herself without complaining. After Anne retired from playing her *Mary Poppins'* role, we decided not to replace our animal stock, but to let natural attrition take its toll. By the time of my uncle's first coming, there were only two dogs, one cat and one chicken left standing.

Snoopy, or *Snoop*, as he was affectionately known around our neighbourhood, loved his food, but not his exercising. He was oversized, cuddly and affectionate. He also loved to snoop around (hence his name). He would often lie in the sun on a winter's day. "Nothin' better," he reckoned.

Shadow, our female tabby cat, had all the neighbourhood toms calling around on a regular basis. Many a time there would be a catfight in our front yard, or out back. It didn't matter whether it was day or night. Given this problem, we kept Shadow indoors every night, and then let her out each morning.

The new people in the house across our street had decided enough was enough with the catfights, so they anonymously hand-delivered a letter of complaint to our letterbox, and to all our neighbours, requesting all cats be caged, as required by local by-laws. They referenced council rules in their letter of complaint. Several long-term neighbours confided to us that they were mystified to receive such a complaint when they didn't own a cat! We felt we were very special because we received two letters, both at the same time. People can be self-interested at times; it didn't matter to them that they had two incessantly barking dogs.

And then there was April, the boss chook who had no chooks left to boss around. April became very lonely when all the other chickens passed away. She would sit at our back door early each morning, wait to be greeted, and then we would feed her. In her early years, she was very standoffish and mean, so this change in her personality was a big surprise. During the last year, we had become very close.

"Could you use an XXXX coldie?" I asked of anyone who was listening.

Kevin put his hand up and said, "Good as gold!"

I returned from the kitchen with two cold beer tins in hand, one of which was keenly grasped by Kevin.

He lowered his mouth towards the top of the can, formed his lips into a small circle, and then blew over the top of it. He followed up this action by placing his lips over its big mouth, had a swig, and then exclaimed, just like a pirate, "Arrrh—that's better!" After sitting back and enjoying the flow of the cold, amber fluid down his parched throat, he then explained, "I likes to blow the rubbish off the top of the can first before I put me lips to it. It's a medical thing."

Anne then piped up. "Where's mine?"

Somewhat embarrassed, I returned to the kitchen, poured a glass of wine for my Annie, returned to the assembly, and handed it to her. Whenever I saw my Uncle Kevin it would always be an unexpected visit such as this.

I sat down in my usual chair, looked at Kevin, and asked, "So what brings you all the way up here?"

My uncle didn't immediately respond. He was in the process of still enjoying the amber liquid and surveying his surroundings.

He looked east towards the bay, and then turned to me and said, "Gee that's a nice cool breeze comin' in from the west."

I replied, "East—that's east. You're facing east." I pointed towards the bay.

"Okayyyy," he said, knocking back another gulp of his beer. "I've got a bit of a travellin' bug at the moment. I decided to head north a few weeks ago to see where I would end up, and here I am!"

I responded with, "Welcome, it's good to see you again. It's been too long," as I raised my can in salute.

"Cheers and thank you," said Kevin, formally enunciating each word.

"Double cheers," said Anne as she raised her wine glass in response to our salute.

My Uncle Kevin had not been a big part of my life. I remember there were about ten visits in as many years. When I was young, I remember when he did show up, he always had that characteristic big grin, a positive outlook, and of course, a good story to tell. On top of all that, he had a facial twitch. He just loved to tell stories, despite his constant twitch. He was one of the more outgoing members of my father's family. He was not prone to partaking excessively of the demon drink, unlike my father. My mother often referred to these *Kevin visits* as *spot fires* that occurred about half a dozen times through my youth.

As I observed Kevin in discussion with my wife, a series of images experienced in my younger years came flooding back.

#

When I was very young, Kevin would visit unannounced, much to the dismay of my mother (Mum was a planner), and then take my two brothers and me for a ride in his motor car (which was a big deal back in those days when cars were owned by a limited few). My brothers and I would give him merry hell by rolling down the car windows and calling out "Assistance! Assistance!" much to the horror of onlookers and the general neighbourhood. Our top speed back in those days would have been only twenty miles per hour.

I remember a visit from Kevin, accompanied by his first girlfriend, when we were living in Sydney. Annette was the most beautiful girl I had ever seen (well, at twelve years old, I thought so), and they made such a wonderful couple. When my teenage juices started to churn, I wanted to find my own Annette, and be as happy as they both appeared to be.

Shortly after this visit, they became engaged and were married.

A few years later, Kevin came knocking on our front door (we were living in Bondi at that time) to inform us that he and Annette had separated. I was devastated. Kevin and my father adjourned to the Bondi Royal Hotel to drown my uncle's sorrows, only to become involved in a pub punch-up. Unfortunately, it was with two undercover police officers, so both were detained overnight at the pleasure of the local constabulary.

In my late teenage years, from time to time, I would visit Kevin and his family. I got to know my uncle very well during this period of my life. Sometimes I would help him with the mechanical work on his racing car. Other times, we would just sit and have a chat, with a beer in hand. I learnt a lot from my uncle way back then.

The last time we broke bread with Kevin was at my Aunt Helen's home many years ago. Anne and I had arrived for a visit while we were in town. Kevin arrived later, accompanied by Julie, his soon-to-be second wife. It was a good night, and I was happy for them both.

Anne and I briefly saw Kevin again at my stepfather's 90th birthday party, the year before this current visit. Kevin could not stay long because he said he had eaten a rotten chicken schnitzel, so he wasn't feeling well. We barely exchanged meaningful words, but he said he would catch up with us *sometime in the future*.

#

The future has arrived, I thought to myself as I observed Kevin. His discussion with Anne soon concluded, so he then asked of anyone who was listening, "What's the neighbourhood like?"

This query dragged me back to the present time. "Good as gold," I responded. "Anne and I have been here since '78. We had this house built and have no reason to move."

Kevin further enquired, "And what about youse neighbours?"

I gave my uncle an overview of our neighbours. I pointed east. "Across the street we have Gumby."

Kevin looked perplexed. "Gumby? Why Gumby?"

"Yeah, Gumby. He's much the same as that plasticine figure on TV. He looks and walks just like him. Then two doors down we have Numbskull."

Kevin again enquired, "Why Numbskull?"

"Because he has nearly run me and the dogs over with his four-wheel drive several times while we were out walking. Then next to Numbskull is his mate Dickhead."

"Dickhead?"

"Yeah, Dickhead, he lets his dick rule his brain every time. And last but not least is Melon-head."

Kevin jumped in. "Melon-head because his head is bigger than his shoulders?"

"Right on!" I confirmed.

"So youse don't get along with youse neighbours," Kevin surmised.

"It might seem that way, but we're on talking terms with them, except for Dickhead. Dickhead kicked his wife out a few years ago and then brought in the same model. We have no time for him."

Kevin seemed lost by this new turn in the conversation, "Same model?"

"Yep. His first wife was a big girl, fat and blonde, and his current companion is fat and blonde."

Kevin joked, "So he's not a progressive!" and we all laughed.

I then pointed to the house next door and exclaimed, "that is the coloured house."

"Coloured house?"

"Yeah—it was built by a fellow with the family name of Green. He was violent towards his wife, so they separated then sold to a fellow and his family by the name of Brown. Brown's wife took up with a young fella, so they divorced. John White then moved in. White found his own house, so he moved out. The house was then rented by a fellow having the name of Grey. Grey and his wife separated so the house was then occupied by a fellow by the name of, would you believe it, Green!"

"That's unbelievable!" chuckled Kevin.

Then we sat in silence for a little while, thinking about different things. The radio in our living room was announcing something about a cyclone that was looking like it may form off the coast.

I broke our little silence with, "How's Julie?"

Kevin came out of his thought-holding pattern. His face turned ashen.

He mumbled something like, "Gee, ya must be a mind reada'."

His voice increased in volume as he declared, "Julie kicked the planet a coupla' years ago. She'd been very ill. I was gunna let youse know at Gerry's' birthday party but that rotten chicken schnitzel got in the way."

Again, there was silence between us. "We are so very sorry to hear that Kevie," consoled Anne. "We didn't get to know Julie, but we are sure she was a beautiful person."

Kevin looked up at Anne with moist eyes and blubbered, "She was, Anne. After I left the coal union, we did a lot of travellin' together—we enjoyed each other's company, just like you two. Sorry I didn't let youse know but it happened so quick and there was a lot for me to organise. Knowin' Anne's condition, I didn't think youse would come down for her send-off" There was more silence. I guessed we were all paying our respects to Julie.

I broke our silent worship with, "You were in the coal union?"

Kevin looked up again and said, "Yep—organiser at Muswellbrook and Liddell.

"From there I progressed to secretary. I've got a lotta' stories to tell youse — good and bad— if ya want to hear 'em."

I thought for a moment and then suggested, "You need to put it all down on paper—the history of the union. Maybe write a book? The coal union doesn't exist any more."

Kevin was silent for a moment, then said, "One day, maybe."

I felt this might be a touchy subject for him, so I didn't press any further. I plotted to find the right time to discuss what I felt was a very important subject. We both fell back into the same silence over Julie.

Anne then asked, "Chris, why didn't you get Kevin to use our new lift to come up?"

"It didn't come to mind." I looked at Kevin and said, "We have a proper 'up and down' lift, Kevie, not a stair lift. Do you want to have a look?"

Anne added, "We call her *Lucy*—Lucy Lift." Suddenly she cried out, "Hang on, wait a minute!" which startled Kevin and me. "How long are you staying for, Kevin—Kevie?"

"For a short while if that's OK? I'm thinkin' of travellin' around a bit, see your area, drive up the coast, maybe look up Julie's best friend."

Anne enquired, "Best friend?"

"Yeah, Amanda and Julie were best mates. They knocked around together for most of their lives—until I came along," he replied with a grin.

"Does she know you're coming?" added Anne.

"No—youse know how I like to surprise people!" grinned Kevin again. We chuckled in unison.

"Do you have any 'on the road stories' you can share with us?" I asked him. "I loved hearing you tell those road stories when I was a kid."

Kevin gave me his Rooster Cogburn look, then his typical grin returned and spread across his face as he said, "Sure can!"

Kevin proceeded to tell us stories of his many open road travels. He had amusing stories of his travels across the Nullarbor, as well as travels heading north, south, east and west. He had been down to Tasmania, over to Perth, up to Darwin, and across to the Kimberley, all experienced with friends, family, or by himself in his mobile home or, more recently, in his white panel van, the same one now parked under our golden melaleuca tree.

There was a recent incident when he was travelling north along the coast road, he said, when, at dusk, it was getting cool outside, and he was getting tired, so he pulled over to the side of the road. He decided to sleep there for the night on his uncomfortable mattress. There were no signposts to indicate to him that a camping ground was nearby, where he would have happily pulled up for the night. At around eleven o'clock, Kevin was awoken by a car pulling up beside his van, followed by several heavy-fisted knocks on his driver's side door.

"You in there. Wake up fella. You can't squat here," commanded a voice of authority.

Kevin sat up and opened his curtain to see a burly police officer glaring at him in the moonlight. "I'm not squattin'," replied a bleary-eyed Kevin in a polite fashion as he opened his sliding van window.

"Driver's licence please," the police officer commanded.

After some time, Kevin found his licence, alighted from his van, and then handed it to the police officer.

"You are Kevin James Odgers?" enquired the police officer.

"Call me Kevie—everyone calls me Kevie!" responded Kevin.

"All right, Kevie, what are you doing here?"

Kevin looked confidently at the police officer, and with his usual grin said, "I'm abidin' by the law."

The police officer boomed back, "The law says you cannot squat beside any road, particularly at night."

"But I'm not squattin'—I'm restin'," offered a smiling Kevin. He then added, "Good drivin' practice says that ya shouldn't drive more than two hours. It's on the billboard about ten miles back. If ya do and become tired, a good driver will pull over to have a rest. That's what I'm doin'—havin' a rest."

This episode ended with the police officer allowing Kevin to "rest up", especially after discovering his disability.

"He couldn't do enough for me, once he realised I had this little leg problem," quipped Kevin, pointing to his skinny legs. "It's lucky he didn't search the van because I had a stash of hoochie-cooch inside."

Anne again became uneasy because she does not like to be involved in such things as illicit drugs.

Kevin explained that his doctor had given him a letter stating that he was using cannabis for medicinal purposes. "Do youse want to see it? The letter?"

Knowing that Anne would remain uneasy until this issue was sorted, I said "Yes."

"I'll have to get it out of the van. I keep it locked up in the glove box," he explained, "just in case someone breaks in or I'm pulled over by the cops."

Kevin excused himself and asked where he could find Lucy.

As he moved off, I followed and said, "I'll come down with you and show you where the guest room is."

"Sweet," said Kevin.

I escorted him to Lucy and then gave him some instruction on her use. We descended down to the lower level, and I led the way to our guest room.

"Gee, this is nice an' comfortable," he exclaimed.

I pointed to the queen-size bed and said, "It squeaks, but don't worry, we won't hear it. The toilet's outside, just like the old days. You need to go through that door, and there's a bath and shower off the guest room for your personal use." Kevin requested a little time to explore his new digs.

"I'll see you back upstairs, Kevin—Kevie," I said as I left him in peace.

After a short while, I heard Kevin moving to his white van. He rummaged through his glove box, alighted from his van, turned, and then applied his usual manoeuvre as he made his way to our front gate. He then joined us again on the front verandah, using our internal stairs for vertical access. He had in his possession the letter he mentioned, and some of his clothes.

"Here's the letter. I'll just put these things in the guest room."

"Thank you," I replied, and then asked, "Why didn't you use Lucy?"

"I need to keep the blood flowin' in me legs. The old sayin' is 'move it or lose it'! I'll be back," and with that, he returned to the guest room via Lucy.

I looked at the letter and then gave it to Anne. "Looks legit," I said as I handed it over.

"What happens if our neighbours smell the stuff, or see him smoking the stuff?" Anne asked.

"Most people around here would smoke the stuff anyway. And anyhow, the letter can be produced if we get raided, so all happy days!" I confidently replied.

Kevin returned to us after placing his clothes in the guest room. "Ya know," he said as he sat down, "the world is still fulla' good people, even those ones that aren't so sure whether they are good or not. People will respond to ya in a positive way if youse engage 'em positively—that's the right way."

"Right way?" I queried.

"Yep," he said enthusiastically. "Youse should never do, or intend to do, a Tony Abbott shirt-front confrontation, but instead give 'em a 'gidday! how's it goin'!' type of confrontation—a friendly confrontation. If ya don't get a response, then ya know there's somethin' very serious goin' on inside 'em, so youse then leave 'em well alone. But most people will give ya a smile and respond with 'goin' good! All right, mate!'."

There was no doubting the very positive approach my uncle has in dealing with people. One of his more recent sayings is, "Always smile today—you mightn't have teeth tomorrow!"

For what was left of that first afternoon, my uncle went on to tell us more stories of his travels on the open road. My favourite was when Kevin was with Julie. He had been away from home many weeks conducting union business. The second night after he returned home, he stayed out too long. He lost time while discussing business at the local pub with his union mates. It was ten o'clock by the time he realised how late it was. He got behind the wheel (he hadn't had too many drinks because he was on medication for the flu). On his way home, he was pulled over by the police.

"Good evening, sir. Where are you going tonight?" queried one of the police officers through the driver's side window.

Kevin looked out his window and said to the eloquent constable, "Call me Kevie—everyone calls me Kevie!"

"All right Kevie, where are you off to so late at night?" demanded the sergeant.

"I'm off to a lecture," responded Kevin.

"It's a bit late for a lecture, this time of night, isn't it?"

"Well," said Kevin, "it's all about time management."

The eloquent constable was perplexed. "Time management? Who would be giving such a lecture at this time of night?"

"My wife!" exclaimed Kevin, presenting his cheeky grin.

Needless to say, he was breath-tested, which returned a negative result. To this day, the two police officers call him by his preferred name, Kevie.

We were so involved in family discussion that we didn't realise twilight was upon us. Snoopy arose from his slumber and was becoming restless for his dinner. Shadow was meowing as she moved through our legs, obviously also wanting to be fed. Elle was scratching at the back door, wanting to be let in, and April was demanding to be let back into her pen.

I turned to Kevin and said, "Well Kevin, I guess you now up to speed. You know all about us, our home and our neighbourhood."

Kevin looked up and repeated, "Remember—call me Kevie—everyone calls me Kevie!"

I suggested to him that he might like to have a rest in the guest room before dinner, and then freshen up. We would then have a before dinner drink, to which he gratefully agreed.

While Kevin settled in for a rest after his long journey that day, I said to Anne, "Your mother was right!"

Perplexed, Anne thought for moment, and then said, "My mother was always right. She was practically perfect in every way. But what do you mean by that?"

"Well, the Friday night before Christmas last, I had a dream that Kevin — Kevie — arrived for a visit. I remember your mother would always say, 'Friday night's dream told will always come true, no matter how old'."

Anne again thought for a moment, and then responded with, "You have it wrong again. Mum used to say, 'Friday night's dream on Saturday told will always come true, no matter how old'!"

"Well, isn't it Saturday today?" I queried, then added, "Let's go and feed the animals."

Chapter 2
A Coming Storm

My uncle returned from the lower guest room after having his power nap. I pointed to his designated seat on our upper front verandah and again instructed, "Have a seat," then added, "Let's have a cold one and hear some more of your road stories!"

I went to the refrigerator and returned with several more, cold drinks.

My uncle exclaimed, as I handed his can to him, "Alcohol! You beauty! No greater story has ever been told with anything else!"

Anne already had a glass of wine in her hand. We raised our drinks and together exclaimed, "Good health!"

This salute became common practice on our upper front verandah each time we sat in conversation, which was most days of the week.

We continued our chat about the weather, family and inconsequential issues.

"Where are you living now?" I enquired.

My uncle's face became mask-like and ashen. There was no immediate response from him. I guessed he was putting his thoughts together.

After a few moments, he came back with, "Me best mate Les and me built a two-bed granny flat at the back of Stevie's place about five years ago. I've bin there ever since—retired."

"Your son Stevie?" I enquired.

"Yep. Steve and I had a pest control business—well, after leaving the coal union, I started up a pest control business, and when Stevie was old enough, he joined me in it," said Kevin. "When I retired a coupla' years ago, Stevie took over the business."

"That was good of Stevie to let you settle on his land," I observed.

"Maybe, but it led to a lot of squabbles, which I don't want to get into," replied Kevin.

"Fair enough," I said, and went on to discuss dinner and what was on offer, and more important issues to Kevin, such as the weather.

At this point in our conversation, my uncle raised the issue of his regular smoking. Upon hearing this, Anne excused herself and went inside to use the toilet. Kevin and I continued with the smoking conversation.

"I don't want to get youse inta trouble if someone smells the stuff."

I responded, very low key with, "Kevie, we have an Indian family — or families, we're not sure how many — living next door. They cook curry dishes every night, so this area smells like an Indian restaurant most nights of the week, depending on the direction of the wind. We have 'Drug Alley' one street back along the railway line, and on top of all of this, the Rebels Motorcycle Club occupies the house at the end of this street. So I don't think anyone in this neighbourhood is going to complain to the cops if they smell your *stuff*."

"OK, but just the same, I don't wanna' have anyone see me smokin'," he sincerely replied.

I moved over to our new plantation shutters on the southern side of the verandah, and then closed them all. I then turned to Kevin and then instructed, "When you smoke, turn off the outside light here and close these shutters. Make sure the door to inside is closed so Anne and I don't get a dose of your happy smoke."

"Good as gold!" exclaimed Kevin. Then he thought a little bit and added, "Will Anne be OK with this?"

"Good as gold," I mimicked.

"I wonder if the Rebels bike gang will sell me some cheap marijuana?" Kevin mumbled to himself. I pretended not to hear this last comment.

I left him to his smoking and proceeded to the kitchen. I had planned our first evening meal together, which consisted of pork chops, baby apple, "smashed" potato (as Kevin called it), steamed beans and corn, all served with a barbecue sauce. Anne joined me in the kitchen after her bathroom break.

"Did you sort his smoking out?" she queried.

"Yep—all sorted."

Anne looked at me sternly (as she does quite often) and added, "I don't—*we* don't want the police raiding us because the neighbours think we've turned this place into an illicit drugs manufacturing and supply company."

Worried about Anne being so worried about this issue, I consoled her. "It's all good my darling—I've got the 'get out of gaol' letter on the bench-top over there. I'll make a copy tomorrow, and if any one comes a-calling, we wave the letter under their nose."

Anne and I retreated to our living room and turned on the television to watch the evening news, just in time to see, and hear, the report regarding a cyclone continuing to form out in the Coral Sea.

"Will that affect us?" queried Anne.

"Not sure — it's too far away for us to even think about yet — let alone worry about," was my foolish reply.

Shortly after, Kevin came stomping in from our front verandah, stepping high, and grinning like the proverbial Cheshire cat.

I guess that's what dope does to you, I thought.

"Thanks for rescuin' me!" he exclaimed in a voice loud enough for Anne and me (and I'm sure the rest of the neighbourhood) to hear.

"Rescue?" I queried.

"Yeah—didn't know where I was heading or what I was gunna' do," said Kevin, still grinning.

"Didn't you say you fixed up the van so you could live in it while you travel around?" I reminded him.

"That's what I'm doin'," he shot back, his grin now gone.

"Well, anyhow, you're here now, and I'm cooking us pork chops for dinner."

"Pork chops!" echoed Kevin. "I haven't had pork chops for a coupla' years—sounds delicious!"

"Here's hoping you like them the way I cook them. Take a seat and I'll get you a rum and cola."

"Rum and cola!" marvelled Kevin. "I haven't had that in years neither! This is a great restaurant to come to!"

#

So for the next few nights, we observed a ritual of mid-afternoon discussion on the upper front verandah listening to Kevin's tales from the open road. Then Kevin would have his smoke while we hightailed it into the living room. When Kevin came in stoked, rum and colas were served (maximum of two each) in the living room. At this time, I would select the evening meal, prepare it, cook it, serve it, and wait for the critical reviews.

"What's there to see around here?" asked Kevin during one of our afternoon conversations. Anne and I gave Kevin an overview of our location and the many attractions for tourists, which could include a day spent in the mountains behind us, where there are great views of the ocean, and several good cafes; a day spent by the sea, a travel time of thirty minutes away; or a short drive to the north or south coast beaches.

"Maybe I should start with some local tourin'. Are there any rivers close by?"

"There's the North Pine Dam about ten minutes from here," I offered.

"I'll check that out tomorrow—thanks."

So then our ritual was slightly modified. Kevin would return from his day of discovery. He would go straight into the guest room to recover from his day out, then he would join us on the upper front verandah in the late afternoon. No matter what day of the week, he always had a story to tell about his day on the road that made us chuckle. Then as before, after several cold ones, Kevin would light up his smoke while we retreated to the living room. A few minutes later, Kevin would come in, and the rum and colas would be served, followed by dinner.

After dinner, sometimes Kevin would pass out, or he would stay awake watching whatever was on the "idiot box" (Kevin's description of the television set). One morning, during one of his local discovery tours, he stumbled across our bowls club, where he stayed for dinner (lunch to us) and ordered chicken schnitzel.

"That was the best chicken schnitzel I've ever tasted!" he declared as we congregated on the upper front verandah that afternoon.

From the time he first arrived, my uncle became very helpful and useful in a lot of ways. We were involved in a special outdoor clean-up to improve accessibility for Anne, given her Parkinson's condition. Kevin ignored his affliction as he provided me with manual assistance in removing rubbish from our yard, loading it onto our utility truck, and then travelling with me to unload at the rubbish tip. We did this many times over the period of a week. Kevin also assisted with repairs to the chicken pen, as well as other tasks around our home. Anne wanted a pathway built to the letterbox so she could "get the mail" each day. Kevin threw himself into this task with much gusto and laid a series of clay pavers to the letterbox from the existing concrete pathway, which leads to the front door. Anne was very appreciative of this new path as it gave her a higher sense of independence.

Our animals readily accepted Kevin as being part of the furniture. Snoopy became very attached to him, and Kevin became very attached to Snoopy. Quickly, they bonded, and no matter where Kevin was, Snoopy would not be far behind.

When Kevin would sit on our front verandah, Snoopy would sit by him and lay his head on Kevin's foot. We invited Kevin to walk Snoopy each day, but only if he was feeling up to it.

"I was gunna' ask youse that," stated Kevin with his usual grin. Kevin and Snoopy became a talking point of the neighbourhood—the slow overweight Snoopy being walked by a high-kicking person who had trouble walking himself, let alone walking a dog. They would regularly walk up and down our street because, according to Kevin, "We both need the exercise."

Elle was little bit stand-offish at first (maybe because she was jealous of the attention Kevin paid to Snoopy), but she quickly got over it, and often nudged Kevin for a pat.

"Might be best if you don't try to walk Elle," I said to him one afternoon.

"Yeah, I can see what ya mean. She's unbelievable! Full on, isn't she?"

"Yep. She would most likely pull you over, she's so strong. And she's so quick—she might wrap the lead around your legs and do some damage," I added.

"No worries—I'll leave it to afternoon pats," concluded Kevin.

Kevin also became very attached to April, the last chook standing. He always referred to her as "the little white hen" (he never referred to her by her name). Kevin could not believe that she was twelve years old and still laying eggs (although only one a week).

"Unbelievable," was his usual comment. He joined in to look after her and would sit with her each afternoon and feed her oats, which she loved.

#

After several more days had gone by, we noticed a change in my uncle's touring habits. No longer would he roam around our neighbourhood on sightseeing missions.

"Seen it all now," he announced one afternoon. We guessed the touring was costing him too much in fuel.

With the reduction in touring came a change in his mood. He was generally down in the mornings, and surprisingly up during the afternoons and evenings. Anne decided not to talk to him in the mornings, because he would often upset her.

Kevin started subtle criticisms of our house, our neighbourhood, and of us.

I would often focus him away from his subtle attacks by commenting, "I wonder if it's going to rain today?"

Kevin lived to talk about the weather, so my strategy would always work.

Each morning, I would go through a ritual of leaving on the breakfast bar a cup for his coffee, a bowl for his cereal, and a spoon for him to use so he didn't have to go searching through the kitchen drawers to find one. I would also leave a part of the morning newspaper on the kitchen table for him to read so he didn't have to go looking for it. He never thanked me for this. I thought that maybe he just expected it.

We found out early in his residency that he has a dislike for Australian football. We were seated in front of the television one night, after enjoying another superbly cooked evening meal (by me), when Kevin blurted out, "What's on tonight?"

I picked up the remote control and said, "Let's have a look!" and started to scroll through the stations. I settled on a channel showing an Australian football game.

"Can ya change the channel—I don't follow that game," yelled Kevin from the back stalls. So I changed the channel. The channel we settled on was a debate about gay rights, now known in this country as LGBTQI+ rights. If the government ever decided whether it was going to ask us, the voters, to help decide the issue of legalising gay marriage, Anne and I were intending to vote *Yes* simply because we both felt that no one should be ridiculed or even beaten because they were deemed to be *different*. It surprised me that Kevin was also intending to vote *Yes*. He added, "No one should be subjected to hate."

After several confrontations with Anne and me over the ensuing days, Kevin took to sleeping in each morning. He would shower around nine o'clock, and then proceed in his white panel van to visit our local coffee shop, where he would purchase his favourite latte and read his newspaper. He would then drive to our local bowls club at eleven thirty, where he would have his 'dinner'. He usually stayed at the bowls club until three o'clock, when he would return to our place, have a power nap, and join us on the upper front verandah for our usual afternoon of small talk.

My uncle's mood swings were starting to worry us. I had to understand the basis of it, because, during the first few days of his arrival, he seemed to be so happy—he had even thanked us for rescuing him. So one afternoon, while we were congregated on our verandah, I broached the subject with him. We were discussing the weather (as usual) at the time. I asked him if he knew why he was going through mood swings, and why he was being a bit confrontational when neither Anne nor I had done anything to upset him.

"I haven't noticed," he said initially, then added, "I haven't been sleepin' well lately—maybe that's it. I tried counting sheep so I can fall asleep, but that got boring, so I started talking to the shepherd instead and that still didn't work!"

When Kevin first arrived, we had offered him the beach room (a room decorated as if you were lying beside the water at the beach), or the lower-level guest room, to sleep in. He had stated back then that "It doesn't matter. I kin sleep anywhere on anythin' at any time—even on a sack of potatoes!" So this latest comment caught us off guard.

"What is it that's troubling you? Money?" Anne enquired.

"We won't be asking for any rent if that's what's troubling you," I added.

Kevin looked at me, and that mask-like, ashen face returned. There was silence. Then Kevin looked up and opened up to us. "I thought I could get over it, but it's causin' me a lot of sleepless nights. When I was in the union, they taught me how to get control of grief, anxiety, depression—all that sorta' stuff, but I just can't get past the *eviction*." His voice trailed off to almost a mumble.

Eviction was big news to both of us. We had not received any feedback from any family member about any eviction to do with anyone in the family. We certainly hadn't heard of any eviction that Kevin might have been through, given that he had been living on his son's property. Eviction is not a family trait. *We stick by family*, or so I thought. A sense of anger passed through me. I composed myself and asked, "Eviction—what eviction?"

Kevin babbled through tears that had started free-falling down his cheeks, "Steve came to me one Sunday morning and handed me a handwritten note that turned out to be an eviction notice. I told youse about the granny flat Les and I built on Steven's property, didn't I, after I retired from the pest control business?"

"You did," I said and waited for him to continue.

Kevin struggled on. "For some reason, Steven didn't want me there no more, so he evicted me. The note was done up like a proper court document, but it was handwritten. And it wasn't Steven's handwriting. He can't write—he's illiterate."

"There must be some reason for him to take such drastic action as that. And who would write such a note? Was your mate Les also evicted?" I reacted, sounding like a defence lawyer not paying any attention to sensitivities.

"I'm just tryin' to get meself under control, so I don't wanna' talk no more about it," pleaded Kevin.

I sat for while trying to digest this awful news. Anne tried not to jump to conclusions because that would have been a useless exercise.

"So from that time on, I've been livin' — and tourin' — in that white panel van," Kevin announced with some pride in his voice, pointing to his van sitting in silence under the golden melaleuca tree. "It's self-contained, has a toilet, a bed, a TV, blinds—all the comforts of home, including solar air conditioning. My clothes are stored in a 'robe under the bed. Since that day, I've been intendin' to travel all over the countryside, visiting family, visiting friends, making friends out of strangers—avoiding any dull moments.

"Youse are the first port of call!" he proclaimed, sounding like his usual positive self. "Ya know, life always offers you a second chance—it's called tomorrow!"

His confession to us that he had been evicted seemed to remove a lot of his angst and worry. I guess it's good for anyone to discuss their troubles with someone who will listen —to get it off your chest, so to speak, before the problem festers. Anne and I have always been very good listeners.

Following his revelation, Kevin continued on with his modified daily routine of coffee shop, bowls club 'dinner', afternoon nap, afternoon discussion with Anne and I (with a cold one in hand); followed by a smoke, then rum and cokes, and finally dinner (by our definition). It was Groundhog Day every day from then on.

The coffee shop staff would have his coffee and tea cake ready just before he arrived each morning. He was as regular as clockwork. He knew all their names, their histories, and their problems. The newspaper lady knew Kevie; the ladies at the bowls club knew Kevie; everyone knew Kevie. From the time he first came to stay, he became a popular addition to our neighbourhood. He would tell stories to anyone he came into contact with, usually our neighbours, resulting in them laughing out loud, which was always the reaction to his yarns.

Several days after his confession, we both noticed he was again becoming restless, and a little bit withdrawn, until he had his evening smoke. He wasn't the usual jovial Kevie through the afternoon, and Mr Hyde was always present in the mornings.

"Anything wrong, Kevie?" Anne asked of him one afternoon.

"I'm gunna' look up an old address this weekend, Anne," Kevin explained as he raised his evening cold one to his lips (and forgot to blow).

"Old address?"

"Amanda lives up at one of the northern beaches. I'm gunna' go an' see her this weekend," said Kevin.

"You'd better let her know you're coming," I suggested, supported by Anne who advised, "No one likes a surprise Kevin — er — Kevie."

Kevin replied, "Yeah, I've phoned her. She'll be home this weekend and she wants me to stay with her a few days— go out, you know, that kinda stuff."

This was good news for Anne and me because we were feeling that we needed a break from him. I guess he thought that too, and that's why he had organised to visit Amanda.

"I won't be leaving until Saturday afternoon. Amanda works up to dinner time, then she has three days off," Kevin continued. The word 'dinner' still confused us when Kevin used it instead of 'lunch'.

"Do you need me to do anything for you before you leave? What, noon on Saturday?" I asked.

"Giving me a hand to fix up the furniture in the van before I leave would be good," he said, then added, "After I catch up with Amanda, I'm gunna' go lookin' for Satts—an old rugby league playing mate of mine from Kurri Kurri."

"John Sattler?" I queried, a little surprised.

"Yep. I've got some leads on where he is, then after I catch up with him, I'll be heading back down south. Prob'ly take me a coupla' months travellin' around up north, then I'll turn around and head south."

Although we were both pleased to hear this news, we could not help but be surprised by his announcement, because he seemed so settled. Sometimes we both thought he was too settled. At times, he acted as though he owned our house, given the way he would just take over—or was that a family trait? Yes, I think so.

Apart from some open displays of ill temper, we'd been happy to host Kevin at this time, so Anne queried, "We won't be seeing you again after you head off this weekend?"

"Yeah, that's about right Anne. I've got itchy feet agin. I need to get behind the wheel and go places I haven't seen before—get back on the road agin. You know me, if I come to a fork in the road, it doesn't matter which route I take, I'll always end up havin' some sort of an adventure!" he spruiked, just to reinforce what we already knew.

"It's been good having you stay with us, Uncle Kevin," I said, as I put my hand affectionately on his shoulder.

"Please! No uncle stuff! Call me Kevie—everyone calls me Kevie!" he exclaimed, and then added, "It's been good stayin' with youse. I do appreciate it. I'll miss the afternoon cold ones, the rum and cokes—and restaurant surprises!"

We all chuckled, raised our drinks and, in unison, declared "Good health!" followed by, "Live long and prosper!"

I directed the conversation back to our discussion about his leaving. "I think the animals are going to miss you, Kevie. No more walks, no more talks—and no more oats!"

"Yeah, I'll miss 'em too—especially Snoop Dog and the little white hen," Kevin said wistfully.

As Kevin was preparing to leave us on that Saturday morning to "look up a coupla' old addresses", I assisted him with his mattress.

"Get that bloody mattress placed flat so it doesn't stick me in the kidneys."

After our handshake, followed by a man hug, then a call of "Bon voyage!" from our upper front verandah, Kevin drove off, heading north along our street. As I waved him off, I felt, at that time, that my paternal uncle had taught me something, but I wasn't quite sure what it was.

No matter where Kevin pulled up, he had a story to tell. Every time he came to a fork in the road, he put his sixth sense to use, and always chose a route with an adventure waiting for him. He met many like-minded travellers, who, for whatever reason, were touring just like him, in a van just like his. But life for him was not always a bed of roses, as we found out many weeks later.

I returned to sit with Anne, who was still waving away with her handkerchief as the white panel van, the very same one she had so curiously eyed off when it first arrived, turned left and then out of sight. As I sat down, the music blaring out of our radio suddenly stopped, and was followed by the announcer eloquently stating:

"This is a community announcement. We bring you a weather warning. A Category 4 cyclone has formed in the Coral Sea. She is positioned 200 kilometres off Townsville, moving slowly in a westerly direction towards our coast. She is expected to reach Townsville in one to two weeks if weather modelling proves correct. She has been named 'Debbie'. We will keep you informed of her progress."

#

Several weeks after Kevin returned to the open road, Elle became unwell. We put it down to Kevin not being there, but then, for maybe the fourth time in her life, we suspected that her cancer may have returned. I went looking for her Monday night after she didn't come to our back door for her dinner.

"She'll show up," I said to Anne as I returned from searching for her in our back yard.

The next morning, before breakfast, I went looking for her again. As I approached our outdoor barbecue, I could hear her sucking in air. She was lying behind the barbecue and had most probably slept there overnight. Elle would always suck in air like that, but only after she had been for a long walk.

Elle loved to swim in our in-ground swimming pool to cool down, so I opened the pool gate for her, and left it in the open position, while I went looking for her lead. My intention was to take her on her daily walk before breakfast. I heard her usual splash as she jumped into the pool—the usual splash she would make as she went in head first. I turned around to admire her swimming, but she was not swimming. She had descended to the bottom of the pool. Without a thought, I jumped in, grabbed her and returned her to the surface. She was not breathing.

I carried her onto the pathway leading to the pool. She was still. I started chest massage. To my surprise, she regained consciousness, raised her head, and then gave me a look as if to say, "What are you doing?"

She lay her head back down on the pathway. She stopped breathing again. I went numb. I cupped my hands, then placed them over her nose, closed her jaw, and commenced breathing through my hands into her nose. At intervals, I stopped and recommenced chest massage. She started breathing again. She awoke for the second time. She raised her head again, looked at me with an unquestionably pleading look that could not be mistaken. It said, "Please, please, just let me go!" So I did.

I was in shock. I stayed with her for what seemed like an hour (when I think back, it was probably only about ten minutes). My thoughts at that time were of the three previous times she had faced cancer and had won. This fourth battle was just too much for her.

She just wanted peace, so I let it be, and she found her peace.

I draped her in a cotton sheet and carried her inside. I announced to Anne the awful news. I placed her in our beach room, the place where she loved to sleep during the day if it was hot outside. I laid her out on the floor. She lay there in her favourite spot for several hours. I sat with her again for a while. My grieving thoughts drifted back to a few years ago when a female employee had lost her dog to cancer, so took the day off to grieve. When the employee returned to work the next day, I remember saying to her, "But it was just a dog!" Karma has a way of finding you.

Anne sat in her chair for most of the morning, just staring ahead, not saying much. She was stunned. We decided to lay Elle to rest in the garden next to the swimming pool, a place where she spent most of her time during the warmer months. She rests there today. I decided to give my uncle a call on his mobile phone to give him the sad news concerning Elle. We knew from past experience that Kevin didn't always answer, and usually did not respond to a text message — something to do with cost, we thought, and maybe his pension — so I left a voice message. There was no response from him. We guessed he was saddened by the news and didn't want to talk.

#

Two weeks after Elle's passing, we were sitting on the front verandah, again enjoying a quiet drink, and telling uplifting stories about Elle, when the evening news conveyed a further warning concerning Cyclone Debbie. The announcement stated that holidaymakers must avoid travelling north.

"Kevin is on his way up there, isn't he?" asked Anne.

"Not sure," I responded. "He said he was, but you know about that fork in the road. Doesn't tell you much—he could be anywhere."

At about the same time, our phone rang. It was half past eight. Normally we don't answer the phone after six o'clock at night, because there is usually someone on the other end of the line wanting something that we don't want to give. I stepped out of protocol thinking it might be Kevin, so I answered with some silly statement in case I encountered a scammer on the other end of the line.

It was my Aunt Helen, Kevin's sister. She spoke in a quivering voice. Bypassing the standard pleasantries, she declared, "Kevin's been in an accident!"

Chapter 3
The Early Years

During those times when Anne and I conversed with my uncle on our front verandah, I would frequently encourage him to write down some of his stand-out stories from the road.

"What for?" was often his reply.

I felt this was an unexpected and strange response from him. He had lived a life most people would envy. During one such story time, I brought with me a writing pad and pen for him to write down his memoir.

He looked at me and jovially commented, "Are ya puttin' together ya shoppin' list? Don't forget the cold ones — and the rum and cokes!"

When I explained the purpose of the pen and paper, he said "Thanks", and that was the end of that part of our conversation. Another time, I sat in my usual chair with pen and writing pad in hand, with the intent of putting down some historical dot points for him to expand on, but he just clammed up. I was disappointed with him, because I felt that it is well worthwhile recording one's life experiences so others get to know about them, and are entertained and educated by them. Stories such as Kevie's also provide positive comparisons with happenings in one's own life.

The following chapters are a recollection of many conversations with my paternal uncle, as told by him in his own words, and as best I can recall. The period spans six decades, from his early childhood to the eviction. Each chapter includes what I know of him and the many entertaining stories he has told.

I start at the beginning of his life. It was late summer 1942. The sound of 'White Christmas', a very popular song sung by Bing Crosby, was playing out of everyone's radio at that time—or at least, those who were fortunate enough to own a radio. The fog of war had descended over the Pacific. In a country town named Maitland, my uncle was born. While Kevin was born there, and also raised there, he avoided living there for most of his adult life. Kevin carried a personal hatred for Maitland, which I really didn't understand, until some stories were told on our upper front verandah at the time of his second coming. One of his favourite sayings was, and probably still is, "Ya can't help where youse were born, but ya sure can help where youse live!"

He would often refer to Rutherford as the place he remembers most. Rutherford is a small village approximately five kilometres from the main street of Maitland, which many locals consider is a suburb of Maitland. Rutherford is a part of the Hunter Valley region.

One fine sunny afternoon, we were again found sitting on our upper front verandah, enjoying a cold one and some unimportant chatter, when I declared, "I don't know much of the history of the Hunter Valley. Who discovered it?"

Kevin looked at me with enthusiasm and announced, "The poms of course." He then went on to say, "Ya know, before the arrival of the *poms,* there was dream-time." He then explained to us what he knew of the local First Nations Peoples, their story of country, and their relationship with the Hunter region.

#

According to my uncle, it is estimated the nomadic peoples (we refer to them today as First Nations Peoples) arrived in the Hunter Valley region around 44,000 years ago, well before European eyes set sight on the country. The Wonnarua people are the traditional landowners of Maitland and its district. A dream-time story from the Wonnarua people explains how the hills, the rivers and the people were created by a spirit they referred to as Baiame, their god. In their dreaming, the valley was always there, though mountains, trees, animals and people were not yet formed. Everything was in sleep state until Baiame opened his eyes, and he, and his creation spirits, began establishing the hills, valleys, forests and all living things in, and around, the Hunter Valley. After first creation of country, Baiame noticed something was missing from the valley floor. Something was needed to sustain the life of the valley he had just created. So the valley floor parted and a mighty river was formed and flowed to the sea. Thus, Baiame's creation was complete.

The Hunter River came into being.

Baiame then gave the people their laws of life, traditions, songs and culture. Some traditions were so sacred they were never to be spoken of to the uninitiated. Baiame also created the first initiation sites named *boras* (places where young boys graduated into men). Once all these acts were completed, Baiame returned from where he came.

Kevin went on to explain that Baiame's time on the land earned him the name Sky Father from the people he created. The laws that were made in the dreaming have been passed on to the people by the sky spirits over many generations.

"The biggest lesson us white fellas need to learn from the laws of First Nations Peoples is that our species — them and us — don't own the land. The land owns them and us, and every other species on this planet," lectured Kevin. "And all species on this planet are created equal. We are all born; we live; and then we die—ya can't change the first or last part, but ya can sure help how ya live."

Kevin went on to say that recorded European history teaches us that Europeans arrived in the Hunter Valley region in the early part of the 19th century, following the establishment of Sydney town in the late 18th century. Expansion of free settlement moved north from Sydney town, where, apart from the rich alluvial plains stumbled upon by explorers, prospectors, settlers and shipwrecked people, raw materials used for building were also discovered, such as stone, and many types of trees used for producing lumber, including cedar.

A very important discovery was made by a shipwrecked family in the early days of European migration. After they made it to shore (now Port Stephens), they gathered wood to build a fire to keep themselves warm and to form a smoke signal. They stumbled upon unfamiliar black rocks lying everywhere on the surface, which they used to form their first fire pit. They observed that the black rocks burned with the fire in the pit. And so coal was stumbled upon in abundance, at the surface, and later, in the ground, and, like gold, caused a huge influx of prospectors and settlers.

Following these discoveries, European settlement of the Maitland region began in earnest during the early 1800s. The town of Maitland was eventually formed by the combination of three smaller towns, which were each established independently at about the same time by the government of the day for prospectors, pastoralists, farmers and miners. Unlike Sydney town, each of these small towns grew separately and without proper town planning.

The original West Maitland township was a privately founded town that grew because of its proximity to the Hunter River, and today it is the commercial centre of Maitland.

The other two settlements of the day were East Maitland, which was established by the colonial New South Wales government, and Morpeth, a shipping port established along the lower Hunter River to ship people and supplies in and out of the Hunter Valley region.

The towns, as they grew, functioned as separate municipalities.

Materials and supplies such as lumber for building, coal for heating, and general supplies were carted by bullock teams through the region to and from the shipping port. Originally, the bullock teams tracked their way, in a meandering fashion, through each of these small towns. The original bullock track became fixed as the route that now runs along High Street, the main street through Maitland. You can see from High Street's meandering way that the teams of bullocks determined its route.

The official name, Maitland, was gazetted in 1885 to include the three towns. The name was taken from Sir George Maitland, the Under Secretary for the Colonies at that time. Today, the Hunter Valley still remains a large coal-producing region.

Rutherford, where Kevin always says he was born and raised, has a long association with sports. Horse racing featured early in its history, followed by other sports such as rugby league. In 1886, a landscaped racecourse was constructed for use by the Northern Jockey Club. The complex was progressively expanded, including the addition of a private rail siding with unloading facilities, as well as two grandstands, each seating up to 1000 spectators, a bar and visitor amenities. This racecourse was also used as a landing ground by pioneer aviators, Charles Kingsford-Smith and Bert Hinkler. The racecourse fell into disrepair following the outbreak of the Second World War.

A National Textiles factory was established at Rutherford following cessation of World War II hostilities. This factory, which Kevin often visited if he was not fishing, was located not too far from his home. So according to Kevie, he was born and raised in Rutherford, a beautiful part of Baiame's Hunter Valley creation.

#

Kevin's home was serviced by the Maitland bus. The local bus would stop outside each house along its route—there were not many houses along the bus route back in those days. The bus line did not officially establish drop off/pick up names along the bus route, so Kevin's bus stop was named

The Odgers Stop by patrons who passed by on the Maitland bus. That route is now the New England Highway, which connects Sydney to Brisbane, passing through Rutherford.

Kevin's siblings were older sisters Josey, Ilean and Dulcie, followed by older brothers Billy, Joe and Les (Les, my father, was known as 'Snowy' because of his shock of blond hair), then there were the younger twins, Heather and Helen. The youngest of the brood was Robert, who passed away at the age of two-and-a-half years from infantile rheumatic fever, which was raging in the valley at that time.

My uncle had an affliction. He often had rapid, uncoordinated jerking movements on the left side of his face. As he walked, his left leg would sometimes swing out in an uncontrolled fashion. My family referred to his condition as St Vitus' Dance. I suspect Kevin also suffered from infantile rheumatic fever, blamed for causing St Vitus' Dance. Unlike Robert, Kevin survived.

Kevin remembers Robert had a strong will and physical presence, even at only two years of age. All of the brothers would play cricket in the back yard to pass the time until dinner time. Robert would join in. According to Kevin, Robert could hit a ball further than most of his siblings, and bowl equally well. Kevin thought Robert might be another Don Bradman one day, but of course, that wasn't meant to be.

Back in those days, the New England Highway was not a sealed highway, it was an unsealed dirt road. You could stand on the front verandah of The Odgers Stop and behold the brown dirt highway heading north, cutting a swathe through the undulating hills, which were covered with fields of grass. Sometimes the hills had the appearance of straw.

Other times, the hills were emerald-green.

The Odgers Stop consisted of a modest three-bedroom home, connected by a small hallway leading into the living area. The kitchen formed part of the living room, or 'the loving room', as young Robert would often refer to it. There was an outhouse to the rear, and a free-standing chicken pen in the yard. The front of the house was only about three to four metres from the dirt highway. Kevin's mother, Mary, would often have to sweep the settled dirt from the front verandah at sundown, after the last bus of the day had passed heading back into town.

From The Odgers Stop front verandah, you could see those same grassy fields covering an undulating land rising up towards the east, and then falling away towards the Hunter River, which meanders south towards Maitland. Cattle roamed these hills. After each rain, mushrooms would suddenly sprout, resulting from a combination of rain on cattle dung. After each rain, the family would spend several afternoons together picking mushrooms for the dinner table, much to the delight of the young ones. Only a handful of mushrooms would be taken each time because there was no refrigeration back in those days.

As a young child, I remember engaging in this mushroom-picking activity with my mother on many occasions. It is a very good way of bonding with family.

The picture of cattle roaming the paddocks across the road from The Odgers Stop gave the impression to the uninitiated that The Odgers Stop was a homestead, but it was not.

The cattle and the paddocks belonged to others. The river is approximately five kilometres from where The

Odgers Stop used to be, towards the east, and it was there that Kevin and his brothers would often enjoy afternoons together fishing for bass, trout and carp to put on the dinner table.

Once caught, most anglers would throw back the carp, thinking it was not a good eating fish, but Kevin and his brothers would turn the fish upside down, blood it quickly, and then fillet it, and throw the leftovers into the river. Mother Mary would then crumb the fillets and fry each on the stove top. Fish, chicken meat and eggs were the staple diet of this poor household, supplemented by oats for breakfast, and vegetables that could be grown out of the dry soil in the back yard.

Kevin's father, Bill (as distinct from his brother Bill) would, from time to time, be able to indulge in a couple of bottles of beer, especially when payday came around. He would take his two large bottles, tie a string around each bottle neck, and place each bottle into the river to cool. He would then return the next afternoon to 'kick back' and enjoy this drinking pleasure, at the same time fishing for a meal to be put on the dinner table.

Father Bill would hail the bus each morning, except on Sundays, to go into town for work, and return on the last bus of the day. Bill's trade was carpentry. He worked for several builders in the town. In those days, there was not a lot of paid work around. No government pension was paid, so there would be many workers going to town looking for paid work. Father Bill literally worked for pennies to feed the gas meter. The local bus would operate after dark only during the weekends, to convey patrons home from the movies ('the pictures', as they were referred to back then).

It was tough just surviving back in those days, not just from human diseases, but also because there was a war going on. It was tough raising any size family through the war, and post-war. Fuel and food were rationed by the government, yet you still had to pay for what was available. You were lucky if you could afford it. Most families had set up back yard gardens to grow their vegetables, and livestock such as chickens, goats, cows and the like to survive by.

The population was not worried by the war because they were censored from it. The government decided to keep citizens in the dark concerning the advancing enemy. Little did the population know of a huge sea battle that was occurring off the coast of Cairns, nor the continual bombing of the northern most city by Japanese air raids. These air raids continued across the Top End, all the way down to Broome on the west coast; midget submarines invaded Sydney Harbour; and the youngest and most inexperienced soldiers were pitted against a professional Japanese army advancing across Papua New Guinea to the north.

The Battle of the Coral Sea was fought from 4 to 8 May 1942. This was a major naval battle between the advancing Japanese navy and allied forces. It proved to be historically significant because it was the first action in which aircraft carriers engaged each other, as well as the first in which neither sides' ships sighted or fired directly on the other.

Although a tactical victory for the invading Japanese in terms of ships sunk, this battle would prove to be a strategic victory for the Allies for several reasons: the battle marked the first time since the start of the war that a major Japanese advance had been halted by the Allies, and two Japanese fleet carriers were severely damaged, so they were unable to participate in the coming Battle of Midway.

The bombing of Darwin on 19 February 1942 was the largest single attack ever mounted by a foreign power on Australia. On that day, 242 invading aircraft, in two separate raids, attacked the town, the ships in the harbour and the town's two airfields in an attempt to prevent the allies from using these facilities as bases to contest future battles. The Japanese also knew Darwin stored in-ground fuel oil for ships (which proved useless because contaminants had leached into the fuel oil over time, but the Japanese didn't know that).

Darwin was lightly defended, so the Japanese were able to inflict heavy losses on Allied forces at little cost to themselves. There is a local story often told around Darwin concerning two heroic young brothers who stood on the tops of oil tanks, armed only with single shot .303 rifles. As the Japanese Zeros would fly through the valley and then rise over the hill to strafe the oil tanks, the two brothers would fire upon them—a single shot at a time. It is recorded that one brother did fell a Zero with a single shot. Both brothers survived the Zero attack simply because the pilots were inaccurate and the above-ground oil tanks were strategically empty.

The urban areas of Darwin suffered some damage from the raids, and there were a large number of civilian casualties, mainly seasonal workers. The first two air raids in which the two brothers fired on the enemy were followed by more than a hundred air raids across the Top End.

In late May and early June 1942, midget submarines undertook a series of attacks on Sydney and the Hunter region. During the night of 31 May to 1 June, three submarines, each with a two-member crew, entered Sydney Harbour and attempted to sink Allied warships. Two of the midget submarines were detected and attacked by the defending navy before they could successfully engage any Allied vessels. The submarine crews scuttled their submarines and killed themselves.

The third submarine attempted to torpedo a heavy cruiser, but instead sank a converted people ferry, killing most on board. Immediately following this submarine raid, the invading warships, after deploying the midget submarines, embarked on a campaign to disrupt merchant shipping in the eastern waters. Over the following month, invading submarines attacked at least seven merchant vessels, sinking three ships and killing fifty sailors. The main impact of this submarine invasion was psychological rather than material loss, creating a fear of a pending Japanese invasion, and a growing lack of trust in the government of the day.

Another part of the Japanese disruption by submarine occurred off Moreton Island, in Queensland. A Japanese submarine sank an Australian hospital ship. On May 14, 1943, the sinking of the *Centaur* hospital ship occurred off the coast near Moreton Island. The *Centaur* was white-hulled and brightly illuminated with a large red cross painted over it. The commander of the Japanese submarine showed no mercy for such a ship. He ordered the dispatch of several torpedoes, which sealed the fate of the 332 medical staff on board; 268 of those front-line responders perished in this cowardly attack. This was one of the most despicable acts by the Japanese on unarmed civilians during World War 2.

The Papua New Guinea campaign was an eight-month arm wrestle which led to the defeat of the advancing Japanese army, and so proved another turning point for the Allies. My wife's father 'Bluey' was there during this successful campaign. The Japanese had entered the war and moved relentlessly south through the Pacific, conquering all nations in their path almost at will. For the first time they encountered resistance in the mountains of Papua New Guinea, first from a handful of inexperienced militia (pejoratively nicknamed "chocolate soldiers" at first), and then by battle-hardened troops brought back from the war in Europe. The "chocolate soldiers" gave the lie to their nickname and fought bravely, facing the invading professional Japanese army and stopping it from advancing at Imita Ridge. The Japanese then retreated for the first time in the Pacific war. No army had fought in such terrible conditions before; no army general thought it possible to stop the Japanese advance, but they did. I am proud to state my father-in-law was part of that campaign.

#

Back at The Odgers Stop, while all this war drama was going on, bath-time was once every few days. Bathwater was not emptied each time but reused. Hot water would be added to the retained water to achieve a comfortable temperature for the next bather, until the water became so dirty that it had to be emptied, and a new bath created. The eldest enjoyed the cleanest bath. Mother Mary and Father Bill were last to have their bath.

Artificial lighting was usually turned off early at night, usually straight after dinner time, to keep the power consumption costs down. This meant that it was early to bed each night for all the children. Father Bill would often stay up at night reading by candlelight because candles were in abundance. They were made by Mother Mary from the animal fat left over from cooking. The outhouse consisted of a small building in which a metal pan was placed in-ground. A night-soil man would call in once a week to remove the soiled pan and replace it with a clean one. According to my uncle, you could hear the night-soil man approaching in the early hours of the morning by the sound of barking dogs and the clatter of the steel pans, and the putrefied smell that heavied the atmosphere ahead of him.

Despite all this hardship, my uncle remembers a happy and loving family home. All siblings addressed each parent as 'Father Bill' and 'Mother Mary' because of the high level of respect they had for each parent. Kevin also remembers the kindness of his mother Mary through those hard times. Often, itinerant workers would come to the front door looking for work, thinking The Odgers Stop was a homestead. Mary would invite them in, let them know the Odgers were no better off than they were, except for the roof over their head, and then invite them to fix this or fix that for food and lodgings, if they needed it.

One morning, Mary went to the chook pen to gather eggs for breakfast and came across an itinerant worker sleeping there. He had no place to go. Rather than scold the man, Mary invited him in for breakfast, which consisted of home-made bread, fried eggs and coffee. She found out at breakfast that he had not eaten in a week. He was so grateful for this kindness, he chopped wood all day. By the time he moved on from Mother Mary's kindness and encouragement, The Odgers Stop had a supply of firewood for the fireplace, stove and oven for a full month.

Many itinerant workers would stay for days before moving on because Mary made them feel so welcome and made them comfortable. The Odgers Stop was fondly remembered by many of them. The result of all this was that The Odgers Stop was never untidy. The back and front screen doors never fell off their hinges, the timber dunny lid was always in place, the stove and oven were always clean, the fireplace was always repacked before sundown, and there was never anything out of place in the chook pen.

Kevin also remembers the toughness of his mother if a worker tried to take advantage of her generosity. Kevin recalls that, one time, an itinerant worker approached the front door and did not knock but entered without an invitation. Kevin, looking on from the kitchen, saw him enter and so called to his mother, "Mother, there's someone tryin' to get in."

Mary grabbed her broom and flew down the hallway, yelling to the intruder to "get out!"

The intruder was so startled, he turned on his heel and, keeping one eye on this madwoman coming at him with the flaying broom and yelling "Arghhh", ran into the edge of the half-opened front door. As he picked himself up, he kept apologising while Mary swept him out the front door with her trusty broom.

Kevin was fondly attached to all of his family, but his favourite was Les. Kevin would often ask Les what he was making or what he was doing, to which Les would always respond, "I'm makin' a wigwam for a goose's bridle!"

Kevin always thought Les' response was deliberately absurd because he had never seen a goose wearing a bridle. As Kevin grew older, he discovered this phrase, often used by Les, was an old English code for "mind your own business"!

One day, Kevin saw Les packing his port. "Where're you goin'?" asked Kevin.

"I'm off to discover Queensland," was Les' reply.
"Queensland? Where's that?"

"Why, it's where the Queen lives!" said Les in response. "It's also a place where horses run free—you can pick any one you want and ride it for free as long as you feed it and look after it."

Kevin thought for a moment, then asked Les, "Will ya bring back a pony for me? When ya come back?"

"I promise!" said Les, patting Kevin on the head, and with that, he walked out of The Odgers Stop, and, apart from Kevin, there was no other family member there to bid him goodbye.

Kevin often thought about that time when Les packed up and left home, and why no one was there to say goodbye.

Several years passed by. Kevin was sitting on the front verandah playing with his dog when a tall lanky stranger, with long brown hair, got off the bus. As the stranger approached the front gate, he called out, "Giddy young fella!"

"Who are you?" asked Kevin.

"Your big brother Snowy! Don't you remember me?"

"Where's my pony?" demanded Kevin, realising Les had finally returned home after such a long time away.

"Well, the sad truth, young fella, is the pony got sick and died on the train on the way home. Sorry about that," said Les.

Kevin found out much later, when they were both adults having a yarn in the local pub, that Les had forgotten all about the pony, otherwise he would have ridden the pony home and saved on the train fare! Kevin never found out from Les why he had to suddenly leave home. It remains a mystery to him even today.

Les' return to the family, brought with it many happy times for Kevin. Les would often tell stories of his adventures in Queensland to the family around the dinner table. It was a very entertaining period for Kevin. He made his mind up that Queensland was the place he wanted to go to.

Kevin realised one day that his mother and Les had a special mother-and-son bond. He walked in one morning after tending the chickens to see Les preparing a chicken for the evening meal. Les was a good cook. He was taught by their mother at a young age to look after himself, including how to prepare and cook tasty meals. Kevin was curious to learn, so started to ask Les questions about what he was doing.

"What are ya doin' Lessy?" enquired Kevin.

"Getting' this bird ready for eatin' at dinner time," Les replied.

"Yeah, I know that, but why are ya puttin' stuff into its arsehole?" Kevin continued.

"This is called stuffin'," Les replied as he waved a mixture of herbs and spices in front of Kevin and then proceeded to push it up the anus of the chicken (it was deceased, of course).

As this exchange was going on, their mother walked into the kitchen. She looked at both of them, and then addressed Les with, "What are you doin' in my kitchen, Lessy?", to which Les responded with, "Just stuffin' a bird, Mother!"

Mary slapped Les over the head as they both laughed about his crude reply to her.

#

Several years after the war concluded, there was much migration to Australia from out of Europe. Italians and Greeks settled into the Sydney area, and then moved to parts of the Hunter Valley. Several Italian students attended Kevin's school, which was a catalyst for racial tension. Kevin didn't understand what all the fuss was about. He had indigenous friends at school with whom he shared his lunch. My uncle saw no difference in the newcomers. They were all people just like him. Kevin told us one day that he has always been colour blind and that racism has been blown up out of all proportion. He concluded during our conversation that afternoon that even the Hebrew and Christian God had chosen a race of people above all others a long time ago, "So why is there a comparative problem"?

My uncle's view of the term *'coloured people'* is that the white race are the coloureds. "Think about it, whites turn green with envy, turn red when mad at something, or someone, and blue when starved of oxygen!"

On the first morning of the new students' arrival, Kevin introduced himself to Paolo, a new Italian student. Kevin invited Paolo to share lunch with him and his friends. He opened his lunchbox and took out two Vegemite sandwiches. He offered one to Paolo, who took it eagerly and then offered half of his frittata in return. Kevin was perplexed. He had never seen a frittata before, let alone tasted one.

"And let me tell youse," said Kevin, "it was much tastier than the Vegemite or jam sandwiches I got every day in me lunchbox. Frittatas put petrol in ya tank!"

So for the next several weeks, Kevin and Paolo shared their lunch with each other, until Kevin decided to tell his mother all about frittatas because he thought it unfair on Paolo that he was eating three-quarters of Paolo's lunch every day.

He came home the usual way after school, jumping off the bus just before it stopped.

This action often gave him a thrill and a sense of command. He was becoming bulletproof. As the bus completed its obligatory stop, he ran inside to tell Mother Mary all about frittatas.

"Can you make these mother? It's an egg base with all sorts of goodies on top, fried in the pan on the stove." Mother Mary took up the challenge and set about planning her first frittata from the description Kevin gave her, and within the hour, had produced one that passed Kevin's taste test.

From that day on, the family enjoyed frittatas served as an evening meal. Kevin once informed us that this was one of the happiest periods of his childhood, but he was becoming restless—for what, he was unsure.

Chapter 4
The Restless Years

When Kevin reached his adolescent years, he stopped growing taller and started to fill out. He was athletic in appearance and good-looking, so was becoming noticed by the opposite sex. Schoolgirls would often alight the afternoon bus with him or walk past The Odgers Stop calling out his name. This attention was uncomfortable for him at first, but, as hormones started to flow through his lanky body, he became very comfortable with being a local attraction.

Mother Mary noticed this early attraction going on, so she gave Kevin many lectures about being responsible and playing the gentleman, but I don't think Kevin was listening. One Saturday morning, while the family was congregated at the breakfast table, Kevin asked if he could chaperone the twins, Helen and Heather, to the pictures to see the matinee session.

"What's playing?" asked Helen.

"*Gone with the Wind*," answered Kevin.

"I'd like to see that!" Mother Mary chimed into the conversation

"Three's company, four's a crowd, Mother. Anyhow, you promised us a baked meal for tea tonight, remember? We'd all be very disappointed if that wasn't on the table tonight when we get home, now wouldn't we, kids?" coached Kevin.

After much debate and some disappointment shown by Mother Mary, she relented, but laid down some simple rules for Kevin to abide by. Firstly, he must ensure that the twins were safe at all times. Secondly, he must make sure the twins were home before dark.

Thirdly, if anything went wrong, then Kevin, and only Kevin, would be held responsible.

So late morning, Kevin and the twins headed off on the local bus to attend the matinee show, or so Mother Mary thought as she waved them off. When the bus arrived outside the theatre, located in Melbourne Street, Kevin organised for the admission tickets. He bought only two. He explained to the twins that he had to pay the usher to look after them because he had to go and 'see a man about a dog', and it was a surprise, so they must not tell Mother!

Kevin approached the usher, handed over the twins to her, said he would be back before dark, "I promise, so we can all catch the bus back home," and then gave each of them a hug and a kiss. "Stay out of trouble," he insisted as he bade them goodbye. The usher gave Kevin a kiss on the cheek and then showed the twins to their seats and stayed for a short while to make sure they were comfortable.

Although rather long for their attention span, the twins enjoyed the picture. After it was over, they made their way to the bus stop outside the theatre, where they sat and waited for Kevin to show up. They waited and waited. Time went by so slowly, until the sun cast a long shadow down Melbourne Street. Twilight was approaching. The last bus before dark was coming towards them. The next bus would not come along for another hour, which would be after dark, so the twins decided to play it safe and catch the bus home without Kevin and suffer the consequences.

Just before sundown, the bus came rambling down the dirt highway towards The Odgers Stop, creaking and clanking as old buses do as it slowed down, preparing to stop.

As the bus stopped, the twins alighted from their seats, exited via the rear platform, and then ran to their mother who was waiting on the verandah for them.

They screamed as they ran, "Mother! Kevin's missing!"

"What do you mean Kevin's missing?" Mother Mary called to them from the verandah.

"He wasn't there when we caught the bus!" they exclaimed in unison.

Mother Mary became a little worried, but not too much—she knew Kevin was resilient. He had good survival instincts. Father Bill had taught him that. Father Bill was not yet home, it was his drinking night, so she told the twins to stay inside with their older siblings while she went to the neighbours' house to use their telephone to contact the picture theatre. The closest neighbour with a telephone was some three miles down the road. Mother Mary battled on over the loose stones by the side of the road as she made her way to her neighbour. If the proprietor of the picture theatre did not know where Kevin was, then her plan was to contact the local police.

It took Mother Mary a good hour to reach the neighbour's house, given the diminishing light and the rough route. She knocked on their front door, exchanged pleasantries with them, and then explained why she was there and how she needed to contact the picture theatre to check on

Kevin's whereabouts. They fully understood and invited her inside.

"He's a wild child, that one of yours Mrs Odgers," added the old male neighbour as Mary entered.

Mother Mary reached for the telephone and dialled the number. A voice immediately answered, "East Maitland Picture theatre. Horace speaking."

"Hello, Horace, it's Mary Odgers here. Have you seen my son Kevin? He was at the theatre for the midday matinee, but it seems he must have missed the bus."

"Yes, I think he did miss the bus, but he is at the stop right now waiting for it, Mrs Odgers. He looks a little worse for wear," replied Horace.

"Thank you, Horace. You know how a mother worries."

"Yes, I know, Mrs Odgers. I've already had two calls from my mother, but I got to stay back to count the money and put it in the safe before I can go."

"Thank you again Horace. Have a good night."

"I will, and thank you, Mrs Odgers," said Horace as he hung up his end of the telephone.

Mother Mary made her way back to The Odgers Stop after thanking her good neighbours and letting them know Kevin was still in the land of the living. She waited and waited for the last bus to arrive. It was running late. As the bus came rolling down the hill, with its creaks and groans announcing its arrival, upsetting the silent night, Mother Mary saw Kevin standing on the rear platform, holding onto the pole as patrons often do, in preparation for alighting from the bus once it had stopped.

Kevin was standing there, waving to his mother, and looking the worse for wear as Horace had described. The bus started to slow down, but suddenly Kevin jumped off prematurely. His forward velocity was far too much for him to handle; he was running at more than full speed by the time he reached the front fence. He somersaulted over the front fence, landed back on his feet, then clipped the low hedge in front of the house, which caused him to lose his balance again (he was doing very well up to this moment, he recalled), and then finally landed flat on his back in front of his mother.

"Welcome home, son!" said Mother Mary, with arms crossed, supported by a steely glare.

Kevin lifted his head, opened his left eye widely (as he still does today when he has something interesting to say) and announced, "Mother, I'm home!"

His mother shook her head and politely replied, "I can see that, son. Are you all right?"

Kevin lay back on the timber verandah, thought for only a moment, and then said, "I think so—no bones broken."

Mother Mary then challenged Kevin. "You've been drinking rum, son. I can smell it. And I can see lipstick on your collar!"

"Aw, only a couple of rums, Mum," replied Kevin in his defence, and then added, "Don't know where that lipstick came from!"

Mary waved to the bus conductor signalling that Kevin was not injured, and so the bus proceeded on its way. "I'll see you in the morning, son. Get to bed!" she commanded.

"OK, Mother," Kevin respectfully replied.

The next day Kevin awoke at sunrise to feel pain across his forehead, across his shoulders, and on both of his buttocks. He realised the bed sheet was stuck to his back when he made his first attempt to get out of bed. This was causing his back pain. The pain across his forehead he guessed was his first hangover. He called for his mother, "Help, Mother!"

"What's wrong son?" she enquired.

"I'm hurt—and the sheet's stuck to me!" pleaded Kevin.

Mother Mary examined him and realised he had collected many splinters of timber in his buttocks and upper back as a result of his circus antics the night before. His blood had dried on the sheet and caused it to stick to his back.

"Stay calm. I'll get you a Becks powder and some hot water."

For most of that morning and early afternoon, Mother Mary bathed Kevin's wounds with hot water to soften the dried blood so she could easily remove the sheet without causing too much pain. She then applied Becks Blue to prevent infection, and then removed each splinter, one at a time, using a sewing needle and pair of tweezers. It was not a pleasant experience for Kevin. As Mother Mary applied the medical procedure, she delighted in saying, "This is God punishing you for disobeying our agreement."

"Never did!" protested Kevin, as he lay as still as he could. "Firstly, I made sure the twins were safe — it cost me ten shillings to make that happen. I used me own money to pay the usher to look after 'em, and all the other times they were with me," he stated in his defence. "Secondly, the twins were home before dark, weren't they? And thirdly, nothin' went wrong. The twins are home safe, so no punish Kevie?"

"I think you've been punished already by God!" exclaimed Mother Mary as she continued to remove splinters while the skin remained soft from the hot water. She conceded that he was technically right, but then added, "No more drinking rum, Kevie!"

"Aw, a couple of rums doesn't hurt, Mother," pleaded Kevin.

"Let all of this be a lesson to you—no more drinking, especially when you're supposed to be looking after the young ones!"

And then the subject was closed.

#

It was the summer of '55. The sound of 'Rock around the Clock', sung by Bill Haley and his Comets, played out of everyone's radio (everyone possessed a radio by that time), or the fortunate few who viewed it on a black-and-white television set.

Heavy rain had started to fall in the Hunter region at this time. It filled the Hunter River catchment. The rain was continuous over many days. An extremely intense monsoonal depression had developed over southern Queensland and was moving slowly southwards. This change in the weather caused a great change in Kevin's personality. He could not go fishing. He could not go to town. He felt confined.

"No young fella should be so confined like that, when all's ya wanna' do is sow your wild oats," he exclaimed to us one afternoon on the front verandah.

A strong and extremely moist airflow hung above the basin of the Hunter and parts of the Darling River. Rainfall average density for a 24-hour period was recorded as the highest since instrumental records began around 1885. Falls in the upper part of the Hunter Basin were generally around 200 millimetres (8 inches in the old unit of measurement). With such heavy rain on already very wet ground, the Hunter River, along with its tributaries and the Darling River, reached water levels unprecedented since recorded European history. The Hunter River exceeded its previous record high by nearly a metre, causing flooding of most low-lying homes, with as much as five metres of muddy water above the rooftops of some. Fifteen thousand people needed to be evacuated—most by boat, some by helicopter.

In the end, this epic flood took the lives of twenty-five people. Some 2000 cattle, and many thousands of head of other livestock, drowned, or were killed by floating debris such as swiftly moving logs. The damage to bridges, roads, railways, and power and telephone lines took years to restore. There was millions of dollars' worth of crops destroyed, so local produce was not on anyone's dinner table until the following growing season.

This epic flood affected Kevin greatly. He could not fathom the loss of life and destruction that he saw and heard about. Friends and people he knew were lost to, or greatly affected by, this quirk of nature. The safety and love he enjoyed growing up at The Odgers Stop, was suddenly threatened. No longer was he the happy-go-lucky teenager the local community knew. He was depressed most of the time. He rejected school.

This sudden and unexplained change in his personality greatly worried his family, especially his mother, so when Kevin announced one night at the dinner table that he was intending to go on an adventure to Queensland, the family was a little worried, but then relieved that Kevie was snapping out of his depression.

#

So Kevin left home, a young teenager looking for adventure. He headed for Queensland several weeks after all the flooding had receded. He wanted to do those things, and experience those adventures, that his older brother Les had told stories about many times at the dinner table. Les left home as a teenager, and had been a drover, a cook, a rigger, a blacksmith and a builder. Les was not formally trained in these trades, but he was quick to learn, and so became a self-made man. Kevin wanted to emulate his brother by becoming a self-made man.

Kevin purchased a second-class train ticket travelling to Murwillumbah. From there, he boarded a bus to Brisbane. He stayed a short while in Brisbane at a local pub in town. There he applied for several positions. He secured a job as a labourer working for several builders to earn his keep. He gained a great deal of knowledge in a very short time. He then moved onto Ipswich hoping to get a position in the mines. He was eventually employed by one of the coal mines' management team several weeks after being unemployed.

At times, Kevin was unhappy because he was homesick. He didn't like the hard dirty work in the coal mines and was badgered from time to time by a union official to join the mining union. To join this union, he had to pay a subscription, which he could ill afford.

He saw no merit in it anyway because he could get himself a job anywhere.

On the job tradesmen and labourers started to use the word 'scab' when working near him. Kevin did not know what this word meant, nor why they were using it around him, until one day on the job, he was confronted by a rather nasty labourer who accused him of being the employers' spy, not supporting solidarity, and taking a card-carrying unionists job.

My uncle was shaken by this confrontation. No one had ever been so mean to him in his life, yet alone chastised him so loudly in front of everyone. He felt very intimidated. He was just an inexperienced young teenager.

During his time in Ipswich, Kevin discovered the circus was in town. He always had an ambition to run away with the circus, so the very next day, he quit his mining job and applied for a position with the circus—and got the job. Kevin had a saying during our many front verandah discussions, "Life's like a circus—you can't help but be happy in it."

While working for the circus, Kevin travelled far and wide. He found out that the Queen did not live in Queensland, and that horses were not free there (in defence of his older brother, he now realises that Les may have been talking about a horse's captivity, rather than its cost).

Kevin started his new job with the circus learning how to cook food. This was scary for him at first because his mother always prepared and cooked the meals. Being a very observant child, he thought back about how his mother would do it and bluffed his way into it because he knew the cooking terms and measures.

Within two weeks, Kevin could prepare and cook, ready to eat, Pluto pups, hot chips (with vinegar), hamburgers (with real ham), and strawberry ice creams (with real strawberries). Kevin introduced frittatas as part of the circus public cuisine, much to the delight of circus management, workers and patrons. Kevin thought after accomplishing this feat, *If only my mother could see me now!*

Kevin was given the opportunity to progress through the circus ranks. He learnt how to rig a large tent. He mastered the process so quickly he became head rigger when a number of circus staff left to take up permanent positions in the coal mines. It was boom time for coal. It was also boom time in building due to the government of the day's push to provide housing for returned servicemen and their families.

Kevin was often given the task of helping out in sideshow alley after all his rigging duties were completed for the day. He would be assigned to sell food at the food stalls, assist at the dodgem cars attraction, or spruik at attractions such as the boxing ring.

Kevin realised at this time that he was a confident public speaker. He had the 'gift of the gab'. He was a natural spruiker. At this time in his life, he obtained a safety certificate and a first aid certificate, each simply achieved through oral examination, so he was immensely proud of himself, especially so because his older brother Les had not achieved these goals.

There came a time when Kevin again became restless. He had achieved many things while working for the circus, but he realised it was a dead-end job. He wanted to do something different, he told us one fine sunny afternoon on our verandah, but we suspect there may have been a woman or two involved. An opportunity presented itself one Saturday afternoon while the circus was in Townsville.

Kevin had completed his spruiking at the boxing ring and started up a conversation with a local cowboy. The cowboy turned out to be a well-known and respected pastoralist who, at the time, was looking for drovers to drive a mob of cattle to Rockhampton.

"Can you ride, handle cattle?" asked the pastoralist.

"Sure can! I grew up with cattle all round me," replied Kevin, who always had a way of embellishing the truth. "I used to eat, sleep an' breathe cattle. On top of all that, I got a first aid certificate and a safety certificate," said Kevin proudly. So he got the job—but then he had to learn to ride.

The muster was due to start in a week. Kevin called on the star circus rider to show him how to ride a horse and confidently control it so he could muster. The circus rider saw his keenness and decided to show Kevin how it was done.

"I don't want to stand in the way of eagerness," she said. "It's your shout for drinks tonight, and then maybe you and I can go to the pictures?"

Days later, and saddle-sore, Kevin could easily pass as a seasoned horse rider, but he was not experienced in riding in the saddle all day. The muster commenced early the following Sunday, at sunup. Kevin learnt a lot on that first day about horses, and about cattle. "It's not as easy as it looks on TV," he told us one fine afternoon on our verandah.

He worked from sunup to sundown each day. It was a gruelling experience for him. He was saddle-sore for a week but hid the pain from his new employer. One afternoon, while he was riding the perimeter, the rhythm of the ride caused his thoughts to turn back home. He thought about his father. Now Father Bill was not only a skilful carpenter, but he was also a trained horseman. He would ride the stock routes when carpentry work was not easily found. When the siblings were small, it was not brother Les telling tales at the dinner table about his many adventures; it was Father Bill. He would tell stories about the overlanders; drovers who earned their keep by droving cattle, or sheep, or both, across this great wide land, from port to city, or from city to port. They would ride for many months from one part of the country to the other.

He was not sure why he had suddenly started to reminisce about his father. Days later he would understand why. Kevin made his mind up that, when they arrived in Rockhampton, he would telephone home, and maybe look for something not as strenuous as horse riding to earn his living.

As the sun set over the hills on that same afternoon, there came urgent word via the bush grapevine that Father Bill was seriously ill. He was hospitalised in Sydney. Kevin made his way into the local town to find a public phone to call the neighbours near The Odgers Stop. The neighbours arranged for one of the twins to answer on his second call.

"It's Kevie here, darlin'. I'm callin' long distance. What's wrong with Dad?"

Helen explained that Father Bill was very ill because his kidneys were failing. The doctors had told the family to get his affairs in order as he was not expected to see the week out.

"You'd better get back here quick before he goes," cried Helen.

"I will, sis, just as soon as I can getta bus ticket. See ya soon," Kevin replied consolingly.

#

During one of Helen's visits to see us, she filled us in on what happened to Father Bill at that time. He had been one of the first tradesman to use the first commercial electric-powered drill. It was a new invention, and it helped to get the job done quickly with little effort from the user. Father Bill was good at it, but one day he was electrocuted and was admitted to hospital. He came out of hospital a week later and seemed to be fine, but he never used an electric drill again.

Over many weeks after the electrocution, Father Bill noticeably deteriorated. Six months after his electrocution, he was diagnosed with kidney failure, and had to travel to Sydney once a week for blood treatment using a new medical invention: the dialysis machine. (Helen told us that Father Bill was one of the first patients in this country to use such a machine).

The dialysis machine bought Father Bill more time, but back in those days, there was no such thing as a kidney transplant. Eventually, Father Bill's kidneys failed, and his blood was poisoning him.

Kevin quit his job and bought the first available one-way bus ticket for home.

Chapter 5
That's Life

Kevin climbed the steps of the south-bound Greyhound bus. He had hoped that this journey would be a quick one as he longed to see his father before he passed. The bus driver cranked up the engine. A puff of grey smoke billowed past Kevin's window. The bus lurched forward, slowly increasing its speed, and then merged into the exodus of vehicles heading south along the Pacific Highway.

As the afternoon sun slipped downwards behind the horizon, the orange disc grew in size and reduced in luminosity. As its colour turned from bright yellow to strong orange, it shimmered and then slipped behind the far horizon. Kevin observed this end of day beauty. His thoughts turned to bygone days spent with his Father Bill at the river; at The Odgers Stop; helping him with carpentry work; just sitting next to him, idly chatting.

Those were good days, Kevin remembered. His father was stern but kind. *He is a good man.*

#

"Father Bill was a great carpenter!" exclaimed my uncle, reminiscing on our front verandah one cool afternoon. "He could build anything outta wood—he single-handedly built our house. I remember him showing me how to build an A-frame for a simple roof construction. I used his method time after time through my life."

Kevin described his father as a quiet man. From time to time, his quiet introversion would be challenged after several bottles of the amber liquid. He was prone to a well-lubricated mouth when partaking of any alcoholic drink. It appears that Father Bill was also prone to 'hyper-focus', a paradoxical symptom of attention deficit disorder. When television finally came into the Odgers household, Father Bill would often be in front of it, seated in his favourite chair, oblivious to all that was going on around him.

#

As far as bus journeys go, this one was the longest in Kevin's life. He could not help but worry continually about his dad. Fellow travellers could see he was worried and upset, so would try to engage him in conversation, but my uncle was not up to being his normal talkative self. He was so sad.

The bus arrived at the first comfort stop. It was here that Kevin discovered a taste for chicken schnitzel. He had unconsciously walked into the diner with the other bus travellers, simply to pass time. One passenger suggested he try the chicken schnitzel, even if he wasn't feeling hungry, "because it tastes so great!" Kevin ordered a small schnitzel and hot potato chips and, to this day, has been ordering chicken schnitzel ever since that first taste.

The chicken schnitzel sat well in Kevin's stomach as the bus made its way through meandering hills, cutting through the bright lights of oncoming traffic. Suddenly the bus leaned to the left. The driver knew the danger of applying the brakes if a tyre failed, so he down-shifted through the gears until a manageable speed was reached. He then applied the brakes very softly and steered the bus to the side of the road.

The driver requested all passengers remain seated until he could determine what the matter was. Shortly thereafter, he returned to announce that the bus "has a rear port-side flat tyre", and that they would have to wait "till dawn" before it could be replaced.

At that very moment, Kevin snapped out of his depressive mood, jumped up from his seat, and called out, "Driver! I'll give ya a hand to fix the tyre. I'm a trained mechanic."

The bus driver strained his eyes to see through the low light in the cabin, and then replied, "We don't have any light to see by. It's unsafe to try to change a tyre at night. We're too close to the traffic, and a car might hit us—they wouldn't be able to see us."

Kevin called back, "I've got a German torch I used in me drovin' days—no electricity needed. It can light up a football field. It's called a flashlight."

The bus driver started to move towards Kevin saying, "Let's have a look at that."

He was now eager to get the repair done, given he could rely on some assistance from someone who seemed to know what they were talking about.

"It's in my port in the luggage hold," replied Kevin.

Kevin and the driver proceeded to the luggage hold to retrieve Kevin's port. The driver decided to go ahead with the tyre change because the flashlight delivered exactly as Kevin had described. With my uncle's assistance, the driver exchanged the flat tyre for an inflated one. They were on the road again, with the passengers "hip-hip-hooraying" as their lumbering bus ambled down the highway.

It wasn't long before another problem presented itself: the engine started to overheat. The driver called out to Kevin, "Come forward for a bit of a chat will ya, young fella."

Kevin consulted with the driver and then theorised, "We might be losin' water out of the radiator."

The driver slowed the bus and steered it to the side of the highway.

Kevin, with his trusty torch, disembarked the bus and looked under the motor. He discovered a small water leak discharging from the bottom of the radiator tank.

"Seems it's a slow leak—musta' bin leakin' for several hours," Kevin explained after returning to the passenger cabin. He called out to the passengers, "Does anyone have any hens' eggs?"

An elderly lady, seated at the front, replied, "I've got half dozen in my carry-on bag. Got 'em from my niece in Springsure for my husband—he just loves fresh Springsure eggs!"

Kevin eagerly asked, "Can I borrow one of 'em please love? The bus driver'll replace it at the next stop."

The elderly lady looked at Kevin with some suspicion, and then said, "I don't give nothin' to strangers. What's your name, young man?"

"My name is Kevie—everyone calls me Kevie," he replied.

The elderly lady relaxed. "I'm pleased to meet you Kevin—I'm sure your mother would like everyone to know you as Kevin! Here is one egg, Kevin, as you requested." She then handed over one of her priceless eggs.

Kevin took the raw egg, cracked it, separated the yolk from the white, and then offered, "Anyone want to slurp the yellow?"

The elderly lady took the cracked half-shell containing the yoke, placed it to her lips, swallowed, and commented softly, "Full of vitamins ya know—can't throw that away."

Kevin proceeded to the engine with the white of the egg in the remainder of the eggshell and removed the radiator cap. "It's too hot just yet," he reported back to the driver through the driver side window. "Give it an hour or so and she'll be right!"

To pass the time away, passengers broke out decks of cards and started playing their favourite card games, or just engaged in idle chat. When the cooling-down hour had passed, Kevin emptied the white of the egg into the radiator, and then replaced the radiator cap.

"Start the bus," he commanded to the driver.

Kevin returned to the passenger cabin and explained to all on board the egg white trick. The water and egg mixture would find its way to the hole in the radiator. The white of the egg "won't solidify until there is air mixed in as well." When the water mixture moves through the small hole, it will mix with the outside air, and harden, so sealing off the hole.

Kevin's egg magic worked. He filled the radiator with a little additional water from the passenger drinking container, and then they were off on the road yet again, with all the passengers singing out loudly, "Hip-hip-hooray for Kevie!"

After many more hours on the road, the bus arrived at The Odgers Stop. This was not a scheduled stop for

Greyhound buses, but because Kevin had been so proactive in keeping the bus moving along its journey, the bus driver, at his own discretion, decided to reward Kevin by stopping outside his home.

There are still good people in this world, Kevin thought as he waved the Greyhound bus goodbye, then turned and faced his family home.

The twins and Mother Mary heard the Greyhound bus ambling along the highway, and then unexpectedly stopping outside their home. They would often hear this same Greyhound bus pass by once each week. It had never stopped outside their home—it always passed by at high speed.

Mother Mary looked out through the front window of her bedroom, where she had been grieving, and saw Kevin alight the bus.

"Kevin's home, girls!" she instantly yelled to the twins, who were engaged in children's activities in the living room.

As Kevin bent down to grab his well-used and well-travelled port, the twins came out of the front door, running as quickly as their little legs could take them to him. They were both sobbing. He knew instantly from their body language that Father Bill had passed away.

"It's OK, girls. I'm OK," he cried, trying to hide his burst of sorrow from them. The twins hugged and held on as his arms enveloped each one. "I know this is a very sad time for us all, but we need to keep rememberin' all of the good times we had. Our father was a great man—a great father," said Kevin, unchecked tears rolling down both cheeks.

They kept hugging each other for what seemed like many minutes. He then said, "Let's go and see Mother." With that, they all slowly moved at mourning pace towards their home.

Mother Mary had put her grief to one side as the twins rushed out of the house and then pushed herself to stand on the front verandah at her position of power, as she always did, to welcome anyone home. She presented a forced smile.

As they made their way into the house, none spoke. When he arrived in the lounge, Mother Mary asked Kevin if he would like a cup of tea.

"Yes please," he said, and his mother obliged. Kevin and his mother then moved on to the front verandah because "Mother needed some air," he recalled.

Mother and son sat there together all afternoon, as Anne and I do on our upper front verandah each day. The twins, not wanting to engage in any sad talk, played in the back yard.

"When did it happen?" Kevin asked of his mother.

"Yesterday, son," was all that Mother Mary could initially muster, being overcome with so much grief. After a short while, she sadly muttered, "That's just life—we need to deal with it."

Ongoing discussion was not solely confined to Father Bill. Mother Mary wanted some relief from the overwhelming sadness, so she would change the subject. My uncle's adventures in Queensland, along with what was going on with the family before and after Father Bill's passing, were discussed.

After several hours spent on the front verandah, talking about death and family, they moved on into the living room. Kevin's eyes surveyed the inside of that part of the house as they sat down. He noticed a few changes, and a few additions.

"Finally got a fridge, Mother!" he exclaimed as his eyes surveyed the kitchen.

"Your father brought it home a few months ago. He got a bonus for working so hard ova' the last twelve months, so he surprised me with it," replied Mother Mary.

"Anythin' in it, like a bottle of beer?" enquired Kevin.

"A coupla' bottles—your father's. He was gunna' go fishing today. You can have 'em if you want," she said in an unfocused way.

So for the rest of that afternoon, Kevin enjoyed each swallow of beer left behind by his father. He raised the bottle occasionally to heaven, thinking about his father each time he drank.

There was no one else in the house for my uncle to talk to about his deeper feelings, except for Mother Mary. Kevin yearned to have a heart-to-heart discussion with his older brothers and sisters, especially his sisters, at a sibling-to-sibling level, but all of the older ones were now married and had moved away. He could not have a sibling conversation with the twins, because they were simply too young to understand.

The funeral service was a short one, for the sake of the family. Josey and family had travelled from Murwillumbah, and Les and family from Sydney. Other family members were scattered around the country. They were on holidays, or just travelling around as this clan likes to do.

This was a very sad period for Kevin.

"The wind had been taken from me sails. It felt like a big kick in the guts for a long time," he would often repeat when discussing the death of his father.

For several months after Father Bill's passing, Kevin sought odd jobs here and there to pay his way in the family home. He did not want the commitment of a full-time position because he could not focus his thoughts. He would often listen to Roy Orbison's 'Only the Lonely' and Brenda Lee's 'I'm Sorry'. But then came Elvis Presley's 'It's Now or Never', suddenly bursting into his melancholy world.

The Friday after 'It's Now or Never' was released, Kevin came home all excited, which was a bit of a pleasant shock for Mother Mary. She would see him, and hear him, day in and day out, moping around listening to those sad songs.

"The boys are goin' into Newcastle tonight to see some live bands, and I've been invited!" Kevin joyfully exclaimed. "Is that all right with you Mother?"

The 'boys' were his best friends, whom he had been avoiding since his father's death.

"Well, son, stay off the rum, and stay on the bus until it stops, then it's OK with me", she replied with a grin.

"Thanks Mum—Mother," he said, then headed to his bedroom to change his clothes and catch the next local bus into town where he would meet up with his friends. He had Friday on his mind. Kevin mentioned to us one day in discussion about the Monday-Friday enigma. He declared, "When it's Monday, Friday seems so far away—four days. Then when Friday finally arrives, it's only two days 'til Monday returns!"

#

Even though Kevin was born a few years too early, he was very much a part of the 'baby boomer' generation (a label given to people who were born immediately following World War II). There is a familiar saying among baby boomers that goes something like, "If you can remember the sixties, then you weren't really there" (it was all about sex, drugs and rock'n'roll). Anne and I are children of the sixties. I remember it was a socially turbulent decade, and I understand my uncle was in the thick of it.

This heady decade in our history saw social challenge mainly driven by the youth of the day because of the perceived sins of their fathers. There was widespread opposition to the Vietnam War, in particular, the government's compulsory conscription law, underpinned by the slogan, "All the way with LBJ". The compulsory ballot (a method of conscripting young men to fight in the Vietnam War) was based on a lottery linked to birth dates. This dictatorial approach by government in an otherwise free society gave rise to continual social unrest, which then led to the emergence of the conscientious objector (youths who knew they would not kill if a rifle was placed in their hands).

Kevin explained it all to us one cold wet afternoon on our upper front verandah. "The government's conscription policy was unfair on everyone. If it had started just a coupla' years earlier, I could've been called up by a ballot number when I turned twenty. Once conscripted, I coulda ended up in that bloody Vietnam war, yet I couldn't vote 'till I reached twenty-one, nor could I enter a pub to drink until I was twenty-one—but I did anyhow!"

Simply put, the youth of the day could not vote to determine their destiny, nor drink alcohol to drown their sorrows. Their favourite chant during these heady days was,

"Make love, not war!" There was widespread use of marijuana as a form of escapism from the harsh reality.

When my uncle had difficulty explaining complex events or situations, he would break them down into simple analogies. He explained to us that the Vietnam War was "a punch-up between two brothers in their own back yard". He went on to explain to us that one brother wanted to be a hippie and commune with everyone (hence the word communist—demonised by capitalists). The other brother wanted to be a capitalist and live in a survival-of-the-fittest society.

"Ya don't go in and punch up one brother for the sake of the other brother—blood is always thicker than water! Let 'em punch each other out, and the one still standin' wins," was Kevin's simplistic assessment of the Vietnam conflict. "It should have just been a conflict, not an all-out war. The commies won—but if ya think long and hard about it, Jesus Christ was a communist," he declared one afternoon.

#

The sixties era, which I remember in my youth, was later referred to as the "Swinging Sixties". The mainly black, white and many shades of grey period of the pre-war yesteryear gave way to this colourful new decade. Many old-fashion traditions, including laws, religion, marriage, and even fashion itself, were challenged. The whole world burst into all the colours of the rainbow. There were many women's fashion leaders, notably Mary Quant, who popularised the mini skirt, Jackie Kennedy, who introduced the pillbox hat, and Brigitte Bardot, whose screen costumes dictated a decade of fashion. New fabrics such as nylon, corfam, orlon, terylene, lurex and spandex were used in new fashion because these materials were cheap, easy to dry and wrinkle-free. Coloured cotton prints also emerged as fashion wear.

During this heady decade, our species walked on the moon. John F. Kennedy, Martin Luther King and Robert Kennedy were assassinated (why? We will never know). A surfing culture (I chose to be a *surfie* in my youth) and the indigenous movement emerged. There came decimal currency, pop art, free love, and construction of the Sydney Opera House. This social tsunami included women finding a revolutionary new freedom with the introduction of the contraceptive pill, much to my uncle's delight.

"Women! I love 'em — I love 'em all — our God is a great architect!" he would often proclaim, but only when Anne was out of earshot.

Rich mineral deposits were discovered in the west and the north of the country, so followed a migration boom, which drove future housing booms. Much to my disgust (because I am an asthma sufferer), everyone smoked cigarettes at home, at social events and in the workplace. Kevin remembers going into a hotel in Hunter Street one night to see a live band. He said it was "like walkin' into a 1950s Humphrey Bogart picture—smoke as thick as rain clouds everywhere."

During this decade, labelled the sixties, I remember sporting success flourished on the court, in the pool, on the track and on the golf course. Margaret Court won several major titles, including the Australian Open, and is still one of only three women to complete the famous Grand Slam in one calendar year. I think it was Margaret's success that inspired the likes of Evonne Goolagong and Pat Cash to become world-beaters on the tennis court. Dawn Fraser won Olympic medals in the pool, which included two gold. Murray Rose was not far behind. Betty Cuthbert was outstanding on the track.

The football codes took major steps forward. At the beginning of the decade, there were very few professional sports players. Every sport was played at amateur level.

Television played a big role in awareness of sporting performance. This focused attention on teams and so increased gate attendance. Advertising and sponsorship rights paved the way for full-time professionals. With this change in our society's direction, greatly driven by Kevin's peers, and later by my peers, there came a change in musical appreciation. No longer did we listen to our parents' music. The youth of the day cried out for something new, a new direction, a musical revolution.

Then the Beatles burst into our lives. There were live performances in this country before they went on to rock the world, and so changed popular music forever. The Seekers found international fame. In the halcyon days of Newcastle night-life, there were at least twenty-two live venues in Hunter Street alone, from The Cambridge in the west end, to The Great Northern in the east end, where live acts could always be found.

Leading live acts included Col Joye and the Joye Boys, Johnny O'Keefe, Billy Thorpe and the Aztecs, Ray Brown and the Whispers, the Twilights, Masters' Apprentices, Normie Rowe, Johnny Young, John Farnham, Doug Parkinson, Russell Morris, and Ronnie Burns. As time rolled on, New Zealand performers moved across the ditch looking for a wider audience. They included Max Merritt, Dinah Lee, Dragon and Split Enz.

Kevin remembers a live band crawl he did with his friends one weekend. They kicked off at the world-famous Ambassador Nite Spot, jiving to the likes of Billy Thorpe & the Aztecs, then went just a few doors up the road to the Palais-Royale to hear Normie Rowe, then across the road to The Family to see a band whose name he cannot recall, then around the corner to the Castle Tavern to see the infamous Judge Mercy, then over to the Workers Club to see Icebox (he thinks that was the band's name, although I suspect it was Icehouse), finishing off the night at Fanny's.

Kevin remembers he fitted in well with the live performances. Being the sort of person he is, my uncle would introduce himself with, "Hi, my name's Kevie—everyone calls me Kevie."

No matter who you spoke to at these live show locations, they all knew Kevie. "He's the bloke who gets behind the drums when no one is playin' and practises", would be typical feedback about Kevie, or "Yep, I know Kevie. He loves to talk, doesn't he?"

One evening, at one of Kevin's favourite live band locations, a lesser-known cover band arrived without their drummer who had called in sick. They invited Kevie to fill in. According to Kevie, he did not stand out in that night's performance, "So I must've done all right if I wasn't noticed!" he proudly declared when discussing this episode of his life with us.

Kevin recalls a confrontation between a young Johnny Farnham and Col Joye (Col was John's promoter at that time). John was in between brackets and Col had gone to take care of some business. Several 'fags' (the derogatory term for gay males back in those days) had congregated around John after their unsuccessful attempt with one of the other singers in the room. They started to chat John up while rubbing his shoulders and his back ("He was possibly cramping from being overworked by Col," recalled Kevin). Col came back into the room, saw this happening and proceeded to scold John in front of everyone. Kevin thought, *One man to start the trouble, one kiss to seal your fate, one kid that needs some action, one link in a chain reaction!*

It was around about this time that Kevin met his soon-to-be first wife, Annette, a beautiful, petite blonde. Their courtship was short, and they soon married. This union changed my uncle's social and musical ambitions, and soon they settled down in East Maitland.

The heady sixties were coming to a close.

No longer could Kevin be footloose and fancy-free. No longer could he be the playboy at each of the live band locations. He now had some responsibility, a wife to look after and, shortly after they settled down, children—Julie, Marcene and Steven.

Kevin was not comfortable living in East Maitland (he detests the very word Maitland), so after a short while, the family moved to Beresfield. The property they lived on had everything for them, especially for Kevin. He dabbled in his favourite racing of greyhound dogs (he referred to them as "pan-lickers"), and then, several years later, speedway racing at Heddon Greta.

#

Heddon Greta racing track was originally a horse racing track. Speedway racing commenced at the venue in 1959. The first track was a third of a mile kidney-shaped circuit. This distance was shortened to the more popular quarter mile oval shape, with lighting erected in 1971 for night racing. This racing venue closed in 2002 to make way for a housing development.

Heddon Greta racing track was only a stone's throw away from where Kevin and his family lived, so it was convenient for him. He would race his red Morris Mini-Minor each Saturday night, to the delight of the crowds.

"I was one of their favourites," he boasted one night in conversation.

The track did not just host Mini-Minors, but also an array of motorbikes, other sedans and sprint cars (UFOs).

During my late teenage years, I remember helping Kevin get the 'red brick' ready for racing each Saturday night. I learnt a lot from Kevin—motor mechanics, body-building and repair. I gained enough knowledge to be able to fix my own car when needed.

The burgeoning responsibility of family, combined with his hobbies of racing dogs and himself, caused Kevin to think long and hard about the future. He decided that he needed a more permanent, higher-paying job. His racing dogs were not bringing home the bacon, nor was he. Kevin found a job with a local builder, then in pest control, and other short-term jobs that just made ends meet, but nothing suited him. He was not content.

After coming across an advertisement in the local newspaper, my uncle applied for a position. The job involved labouring at a new coal-fired thermal power station being constructed in the Hunter Valley. This position would involve travel, and staying away from home for short periods, but he was prepared to sacrifice his time so he and Annette could get ahead of debt. After a successful interview, Kevin was offered a position as rigger with one of the commissioned builders on the job site. He would be required to work eleven hours a day, six days a week, and it was compulsory to join a union.

The 66-hour week was no problem for him; he would stay locally in a hotel, and travel home late Saturday afternoons, returning to the construction site early each Monday morning. Joining a union had him troubled after his Queensland experience. He thought long and hard about it; he could not avoid it—it was one of the construction site requirements. If he did not join, he would not have a job. Kevin was ignorant of the role unions play in society, so he started asking around, discussing his concerns with friends and people he could trust to give an honest response.

From these many verbal discussions over a beer or a coffee (usually a beer), my uncle learnt much of the history of unions, and the relevance of a respectful boss and worker relationship. Kevin discovered from these many discussions that the first respectful relationship between a boss and workers started way back in 1840.

Chapter 6
Union Matters

It was Sunday. Just after noon. We were on our upper front verandah avoiding the sun's rays as it rose to its zenith. There was not a cloud in the sky. Our golden melaleuca tree was swaying to a gentle breeze coming in off the bay. I was reading our local newspaper while Anne and Kevin were in general conversation. The newspaper headline read, *UNIONS PLAN TO STRIKE OVER LOW WAGE CONDITIONS*.

I wanted to start a conversation with my uncle, to get him thinking about his contribution to life, particularly the time he spent in union management. He was never motivated to write about himself. I was hoping that general discussion around this topic may start him thinking about recording his history.

As we enjoyed our usual cold ones, I blurted out, not knowing how to tactfully frame my question, "Kevie, what do you know about unions?"

He turned his head and looked at me, with reservation on his face, then asked, "Why do ya wanna know?"

I cautiously chose my words so as not to spook him. I held up the front page of the newspaper to show him the headline, and then said, "It's been in the papers recently. There's a lot of trouble brewing around the country. The bigger unions are stirring because the big end of town is supposedly making squillions — and paying their bosses millions — but workers' wages haven't risen since the financial crash. I experienced a lot of union thuggery in my early days—I'm not a fan of unions."

Kevin had spent many years on the union side of the fence, so I was curious. I'd experienced much union violence in my day. I wanted to know if he was a militant, or did he display a more conciliatory approach? I proceeded to tell my story that early afternoon, which was a bit of a surprise for Anne, because, as far as she was concerned, Kevin was the afternoon storyteller. She and I were always the listeners.

#

I started my working life as a trade's assistant fire sprinkler fitter. This meant I was a card-carrying unionist. My time on the union side of the fence was short because I was promoted to an office position, so I didn't need to be a member of any union.

As the wheel of time rolled on, I was promoted to project manager. In this new role, I would have to face off with workers many times, which I didn't like at all.

The confrontations I had with workers were mostly concerning minor issues, and the verbal altercations played out the same each and every time—them screaming at me, with me listening and trying hard not to join in their level of anger. There was one time, I remember, when it turned into a physical confrontation.

For some reason, the smallest of all of the unions, the Plumbers and Gas Fitters Employees Union, wanted to be recognised as the first workers union to achieve a 38-hour working week. They ignored the Council of Trade Union's directive not to act individually on working hours matters, because there was a union submission for consideration by the Arbitration Commission.

One Friday, late morning, the workers decided to down tools. They headed to the local pub for a lunchtime meeting. I remember becoming nervous at this sight, because I overheard several workers discussing their many possible disruptive strategies. I was finalising my end-of-week planning report when half a dozen alcohol-fuelled workers began congregating outside my office door. The leaders were the dreaded MacCormack brothers, each one ugly with drink, baying for my blood. I expected the worst and I got it.

I always had a very trusting relationship with each of them, yet here they were now collectively calling me by name and yelling, "Come outside, you two-faced bastard!" They would then chant, "We hate bosses!"

It concerned me greatly they didn't realise that I was just a worker too. I was not the boss. After a short time, I locked the front door. They became frustrated, so proceeded to kick in the locked door. They burst into my office and surrounded me. I told them I didn't have the magic wand to make all their demons go away, so they pinned me up against the office wall.

One of them had their hand to my throat as they yelled any obscenity that came into their angry minds. Luckily for me, an office worker, located in a rented office next door, heard the rowdy mob outside and called the police. The angry mob fled when they were told by the concerned office worker that "The cops are comin'!"

#

My uncle became very interested in my story. He sat up, straightened his back, his eyes widened, and his grin became full, as he said, "Let me tell youse a story or two of who I think the first ever boss was in this country, why unions are necessary, why they matter, and why there needs to be full cooperation between boss and worker. To cap it all off, Henry Ford — a boss — introduced the 40-hour week for all his employees!"

Anne replied with, "Aaahh, good!" obviously thinking my story was not as good as any of my uncle's and knowing that Kevin was far more entertaining than me. Anne became focused with ears ready, and added, "We like to hear you tell your stories, Kevie."

That afternoon was a big history lesson for both of us. Kevin started his lesson with discussion about a man named Horatio Wills, whom my uncle considers to have been the first free settler boss in this country. Horatio was the son of a convict but was not born into servitude. Together with his wife and children, they overlanded sheep and cattle from Sydney town, the place of his birth, to the Grampians (now the Port Phillip Bay District). The Wills family was among the first free settlers in the new southern frontier.

Kevin recalled how Horatio befriended a local indigenous tribe in a very unusual way.

It was his first meeting with them when he was out horse riding. He was surveying his property, planning for the future, when he was set upon by spear-throwing aborigines. Horatio dismounted his horse, picked up one of the spears thrown at him, and then made an attempt to throw it back, but nearly speared himself in the process. He started laughing at his ineptness and so did the attackers. After this minor confrontation, Horatio became popular with the local indigenous tribes. A lasting friendship was forged on that day.

My uncle went on to explain that Horatio showed kindness to the local indigenous tribes. He made an attempt to understand their ways, not like most other free settlers, who trespassed over country. After a period of friendly interaction, he hired some of them to construct a large house under his guidance, on a property he then named 'Lexington'. He paid them well with food, medicines, tools and lodgings. Occasionally he would offer them a cow or a sheep to take back to their camp to share with their mob. When the work on the homestead was completed, the workers were then retained as station hands and harvesters. Horatio continued to pay them well with food, medicines, tools, lodgings and friendship.

"During 1852, Horatio sold Lexington because it was too small for his growin' pastoral an' farmin' industry," lectured Kevin, "so his growin' family — an' the mob of First Nations peoples he retained — moved to a bigger property he named 'Belle-Vue' in Geelong, south-east of the Grampians. Horatio also hired Chinese workers to help with the construction, drovin', harvestin', cookin' and cleanin'. There was mutual respect between boss an' worker. The union between boss an' worker was an association that was mutually rewardin'. It generated an age of prosperity for all at Belle-Vue," Kevin concluded.

"So what happened to them—the Wills family?" I asked.

Kevin went on to explain that, at about the time Belle-Vue was constructed, there were persistent rumours regarding the presence of gold in the colony. The government of the time purposely kept all findings secret for fear of disorganisation within the young colony. They feared that flocks would become unattended, drovers would desert their teams, and farmhands would leave crops unattended. There would then follow a total collapse of primary industry.

By the time Belle-Vue was occupied and running as a positive going concern, gold was stumbled upon in and around Bathurst, north of Geelong. The news was made public by the successful prospectors. This discovery spread like wildfire. A race to reach the gold fields ensued, not just by the locals in the colony, but also by people from around the known world. Merchants, lawyers, entire ship crews, captains included, marched off to seek their fortunes. Each one of the Belle-Vue workers was part of this defection to the gold fields, leaving Belle-Vue unmanageable.

"The moral to this Wills story," surmised Kevin, "is that bosses can't exist without workers, and workers can't exist without bosses. They need each other. They fully rely on each other. Prosperity for all just can't exist unless there are bosses an' workers in cooperation, with respect for each other. Treat a worker the right way, and then bosses will always kick goals."

Kevin continued with his boss-and-worker narrative. He went on to tell us that the first European settlement was nothing more than a penal colony full of convict free labour.

Convicts were transported from England for seven years' servitude, without pay, and at times with awful working and sleeping conditions. Each convict worked long hours, either for the colony administration or for private landowners. They started work as their eyes opened in the morning, and they finished their work when they retired to bed. At this time of colonisation, any servant conspiring to join with other servants, for the purpose of improving working conditions, was outlawed by British rule.

As the colony grew, free settlers immigrated to this new land of opportunity. Some acquired land upon arriving and then employed workers to tend their flocks and lodgings. Other immigrants had no money when they arrived, so they used their skills in trades such as carpentry, stone masonry, butchering, baking or candlestick-making to generate an income. Others were miners who set out through the new land to discover their fortune in gold, silver, copper or tin.

My uncle explained that, back in those early days of colonisation, the law was British and heavily biased towards the government of the colony and private employers, so designed to discipline employees and repress any union of workers, because any union would be a restraint on trade. British law required total obedience and loyalty from servants.

"In simple terms," said Kevin, "bosses owned any worker's soul. Any small infringement by a worker, or disobedience, was a criminal offence punished by gaol or hard labour—or both."

As time rolled on, British law was liberalised, after a series of strikes in England and around the colonies. Workers in England were first to withdraw their labour, and then elsewhere, in protest of harsh working conditions.

"Shortly thereafter, the Trade Union Act came into existence," narrated Kevin.

It is recorded that, during the late 1870s, small trade unions, shearers unions and workers unions began to form around the colony. These small unions consisted mainly of highly skilled workers who sought union with like skilled workers to increase their low wages and reduce their lengthy working hours. These small unions didn't achieve much because of the existence of the Master and Servant Act, gazetted in the colony of New South Wales. Bosses were empowered, by this law, to ignore the Trade Union Act and forfeit wages if the written or unwritten contract for work was unfulfilled. Workplace absence was also punishable by imprisonment of up to three months, with or without hard labour.

"I'm sure bosses of today would love to re-enact this act!" exclaimed Kevin. "Within the Melbourne jurisdiction, when labour shortages were acute, it's recorded that more than a fifth of prison inmates were convicted under the New South Wales Master and Servant Act for offences like leavin' their place of work without permission an' bein' found in pubs. Truly, at this time, workers had it bad!"

He explained that there were also penalties for anyone, not just a worker, who harboured, concealed or re-employed a servant who had deserted, absconded or absented himself from duty implied in the contract. Under this same Act, workers who were absent from their employer without permission were subject to being hunted down under the Bush Rangers Act. As little as a one-hour absence by a free servant without permission could precipitate a punishment of prison or being sent off to the treadmill.

My uncle's summary of this part of history was, "So the moral to this workers story is that workers cannot be treated like slaves. If ya do, then ya wind up not getting' the best out of 'em. Acceptable workin' conditions and hours lead to happy workers, and happy workers lead to prosperity for all. Horatio's story is a great example of a boss and his workers livin' and workin' in harmony. One cannot do without the other—but then there was the greed for gold, and that's a different story."

"How do you know all this historical stuff?" I queried.

"Well, I know a lotta' people because I do a lotta' travellin'. And as youse know, I love to have a chat with people. I get them to open up. I've met heaps of workers, bosses, historians, arbitrators in me day. When they get to know I used to be a secretary of a union, the discussion then swings to the boss-worker relationship. There's a lotta' history out there."

Kevin went on to explain how the union, of which he was secretary for several years, came into existence. The Shearers Union amalgamated with the General Labourers Union, which evolved into the Workers Union. This union then absorbed a number of other unions in the pastoral, mining and timber industries to form the Federated Mining Employees Association, since these industries were the principal sources of wealth in the 19th century. This union had over 35,000 members at its peak, so became the strongest bargaining voice for workers. Direct action by striking became commonplace.

The great shearers strike, and the maritime strike, both in the early 1890s, brought the colonies to their knees. The defeat of these two strikes by the bosses and government caused the Workers Union to reject direct strike action. Arbitration has been a force for moderation in the union movement ever since.

"The whole system had to go national to give commonality to the boss-worker relationship," said Kevin. The federation of the former British colonies into one country in 1901 led to the establishment of the national arbitration system.

"Did youse know the word 'Australia' was not readily known until Federation in 1901? So 'Australia Day' should be celebrated on New Years' Day, the factual birth of this nation."

He went on to explain that the Workers Union strongly supported arbitration as a mechanism of resolving industrial disputes without resorting to strike action. "The Pastoral Industry Award — negotiated by the Workers Union — was the first federal award granted after Federation."

With the shift in employment from the pastoral industries to the manufacturing and service sectors, caused by urbanisation, the Workers Union's political influence and power declined because the pastoral areas became less significant in terms of worker numbers. This decline caused rural workers to fall to the conservative side of politics, and in particular to the Country Party.

In recent years, the Workers Union has sought to modernise and broaden its membership beyond its declining traditional base. Today it represents workers in the metals, aviation, oil and gas, mining, construction, food-processing and retail industries, as well as its traditional base in the pastoral and mining areas.

"So you were part of the 38-hour week campaign—but on the wrong side!" chuckled Kevin. Then he looked at me very seriously, as if I was a boss. "Do ya know we were the first in the world to campaign and get the 40-hour week?" he boasted.

I was not sure if his reference to "we" included me, so I asked, "More information please?"

"This will blow ya away if ya don't already know it," said Kevin. "It was Henry Ford's idea — yep, he was a boss — it was his idea for shorter workin' hours. He believed that workin' more than forty hours a week was bad for a manual worker's health, so the campaign for a 40-hour week started."

I puzzled, "Henry Ford? The Ford motor car, Henry Ford?"

"Yeah—a boss," returned Kevin, supported by his usual grin.

Kevin further explained that, during the 1800s, most workers were on the job for up to sixteen hours a day, six days a week. There was no sick leave, no holiday leave, and bosses could sack workers at any time without giving any reason at all. In 1855, the Australian Stonemasons Society issued an ultimatum to their employers that in six months' time, masons would only work an eight-hour day due to exhaustion caused by the arid climate of this country.

It took further campaigning and struggles by trade unions around this country to extend the reduction in hours to all workers, not just the trades. In 1916, the Eight Hours Act was passed, granting the eight-hour working day to a wide range of workers. The Commonwealth Arbitration Court gave approval for the 40-hour, five-day working week nationally, beginning on 1 January 1948. "As ya know, most workers now work 35 to 38 hours a week these days, thanks to the unions—and Henry!" declared my uncle.

He summarised his afternoon lecture with, "Body science has shown that ya decline in ya physical and mental abilities after workin' for more than eight hours. Finally, the bosses now agree that they don't want declinin' production caused by fatigue. Fatigue can lead to concentration lapses, which can lead to accidents and sick days, or even mental problems, so the power is back to centre—the power is balanced."

"Power?", I asked. "What do you mean by power?"

"It's always been about power—and power shift. The government and the bosses had all the power when the colonies were around. Convicts and free workers had no power.

"Then unions were formed, and the power shifted until it became balanced, 'cause bosses and workers both agree that a 40-hour week is optimum for a worker before manual production starts to decline," concluded Kevin. "And that's why unions matter."

I then understood from that afternoon's history lesson that my uncle was very conciliatory when it came to union business.

"How did you become secretary of a union?" I asked.

"It's a long story, but I'll try an' keep it short," said Kevin, because he wanted to have his smoke. He went on to tell us this short story. "I saw an ad in the local rag for several labourers to work on a new coal-fired thermal power station being constructed just up the road, so I applied. But I didn't get a labourer's job, I got a rigger's job. It paid much more and was less strenuous, but I had to travel a lot. We needed the job to get us out of debt, so I would get up before dawn on Mondays and be at the site by sunup, then on Saturdays,

I'd travel home to spend one day a week with my family. It became a big burden, so I started lookin' around for somethin' else. One day at a stop work meetin', I was introduced by the union secretary to the union president. My life changed for the better from then on."

Kevin explained that he had to attend many stop-work meetings, which he didn't like, because it robbed him of his wages. The spruiking he had learnt to do in sideshow alley became very useful. He spruiked a lot at the stop-work meetings, intending to avoid a strike, otherwise no one was paid. They all needed the money to pay their bills. At one such stop-work meeting, the president of the union was in attendance to give a report to the members concerning a recent Arbitration Commission ruling, and saw, and heard, first-hand, my uncle's unique ability to sway a crowd of angry workers.

A short time after the stop-work meeting, the union secretary introduced the president to Kevin. "Kevin, meet John Maitland," announced the secretary.

Kevin thought, *How unusual! This fellow has the same name as the town I was born in, and I think he is the same fellow I met on a coal site in Queensland.*

Maitland held out his hand to Kevin and said, "You know how to handle a crowd young fella! Where did you learn that from?"

Kevin replied, "Comes natural to me, plus I did some sideshow spruikin' in a circus when I was younger," adding this comment to his firm handshake.

"I like a man who knows how to shake someone's hand, young fella," said Maitland, passing a judging eye over Kevin.

"Kevie—everyone calls me Kevie, please call me Kevie," said Kevin, beaming from ear to ear.

"Have we met?" enquired Maitland.

"Not sure," said Kevin, not wanting Maitland to think negatively of him, so not divulging their earlier meeting in Queensland.

"OK then, Kevie," said Maitland. "I've got a job for you. I want you to train to take over the secretary's role. He's movin' on to bigger and better things for us. So what do you think of that, Kevin—Kevie?"

Kevin was overcome. He replied, "I don't want to sound disrespectful or anythin', but what does a secretary do?"

Maitland called over his secretary, and said, "Tom — sorry, Frank! — explain what your job is to Kevin, ah Kevie here."

"Well, let's see, John," said Frank, fingering the whiskers on his chin. "First thing is to organise meetings: general meetings, stop-work meetings and such like. I take the minutes. I use the telephone a lot. I keep the union records. I attend the court hearings... I take the minutes," summarised Frank.

"Kevie, I'd like you to come to the union office next week to discuss my offer further— see how the union operates at the office level. What do you think?" coaxed Maitland.

"I'll think a bit about it. I need to talk this over with me wife. How much does the job pay and is there travel involved?" queried Kevin.

"That's what I like about you Kevin — Kevie — straight to the point, direct, no bullshit about you. I'll go see your employer and let them know you will not be in next Friday or

Saturday, you'll be on union business. We'll meet next Friday in my office. Frank will tell you how to get there. How does that sound? You'll then have enough time to talk it over with the missus."

Kevin stalled for a moment, taking it all in, and then said, "Sounds all right with me, but can you tell me how much the job pays? And what about the travel?"

Maitland again looked Kevin up and down and all over, then snorted, "Double what you're earnin' right now, son. Union business is mostly done by the local organisers, so travel is minimal, but you'll have to spend a lotta' time on the phone. I see that won't be a problem—you have that spruiking ability that I'm lookin' for."

With his companions, Kevin travelled back home that Saturday afternoon after his meeting with the union bosses. As the sun cast long shadows across the highway, and then started to disappear behind some old grey hundred-year-old timber sheds, Kevin continually stared out through the car window. He wasn't his usual outgoing, talkative self, which had his companions worried.

"You crook or somethin', Kevie?" asked one.

"What's up?" asked another.

"Just doin' a lot thinkin' lately," replied Kevin.

Kevin felt he had to share the news of the last few days with someone; he couldn't wait until he arrived home, and then have to wait for the right time to discuss the union job offer with his wife. So he opened up to his companions as the highway lighting automatically turned on to light their way home. They appreciated his openness and willingness to discuss his personal issue with them. They all joined in to give Kevin their view of the world; the pros and cons of the union position; how his life would change; why they would no longer see him on the job. The senior member of the group summarised what Kevin should do, after sitting back and listening to the points of view of all of his companions: "There is a tide in the affairs of men—when taken at the turn leads onto fortune Kevie," he misquoted.

Kevin arrived at that pre-ordained Friday morning meeting, looking the worse for wear.

"Everything all right, Kevie?" asked a concerned Frank, and he and Maitland waited for Kevin's response.

"I haven't been sleepin' real well since we met last. Lots to worry about and thinkin' lots about this job offer—to take it or not. My wife Annette is totally against it, but I'd very much like to have a crack at it," said a hesitant Kevin.

"OK then," said Maitland, "let's have a cuppa and talk this thing through."

According to Kevin, John Maitland was a very smooth talker. He possessed a high level of skill in organising and then arguing problematic issues in a positive way. He was a very good manipulator.

"So with those qualities — I guess that's why he was president — he had me totally convinced, and I fell totally under his spell," said Kevin. "I didn't know there mighta' been corruption goin' on," he added.

They spent about an hour together discussing Kevin's dilemma, and by the time that hour had expired, Maitland had Kevin absolutely convinced that he had to take the job, but Kevin still had a single big issue to overcome.

"Bein' secretary sounds like a dream job, but I can't take it," said Kevin, dropping his head.

"Why not?" a disappointed Maitland and Frank moaned in unison. They were both puzzled by Kevin's rejection of the role at the last minute.

"I can't take the job 'cause I can't read nor write. I left school when I was very young, so didn't pick up on all that stuff—I'm illiterate," was Kevin's nervous response.

There was silence in the room for what seemed like many minutes, and then Maitland announced, "Well, we'll see if Clyde Cameron can fix that."

Chapter 7
The Second Coming

Our telephone rang. It was eight thirty p.m. We don't usually answer our telephone after six because callers after that time are usually scammers, telemarketers, or worse, politicians soliciting their constituents for support in the upcoming election. I prepared myself to give the caller a dose of confusion. I picked up the telephone.

I could hear heavy breathing at the other end of the line, so I declared, "Hello! City mortuary! Doctor Slaughter speaking"

It was Aunt Helen. She chose to ignore my sick humour, bypassed her standard pleasantries and declared, with a quivering voice, "Kevin's been in an accident!"

"Accident? What sort of accident?" I stammered, having no time to organise logical thought. My mind jumped all over the place. *A road accident? Has he fallen over? Has he been run over?*

Helen went on to explain, "Heather got a call this morning. I don't know any details—someone in Ballina called her," she said.

"I'll give his mobile phone a try. Will call you back once I know something," I offered, trying to take control of the situation.

"Thanks, but you know how he doesn't like to answer!" was Helen's reply as she hung up her end of the phone.

"What's going on?" asked Anne as I returned to our verandah.

"My uncle Kevin has been in some sort of accident in Ballina—at least he hasn't been caught up in that Cyclone Debbie devastation," I answered. "I'm going to see if he answers his phone."

I went about our house looking for our address book. *Bloody thing! I always have trouble trying to find that bloody book!* I belly-ached to myself as I moved around the living room. I called back to Anne as I moved into the dining room, "Have you seen the address book?"

Anne shouted back, "It's here—it was right under your nose!"

Like most mere males, I am predominately visual. I have that male problem of not being able to find anything that I can't picture in my minds' eye. My senses have never supported me (Anne tells me that all the time). When I go looking for an object, I tend to visualise that object. If there's no match with the picture in my mind's eye, then I can't find what I'm looking for.

"Thanks," I said as I sat down and commenced dialling Kevin's mobile number, not expecting any response. I knew it would be pointless leaving a message as he never checks his voicemail.

Kevin answered with a melodious, "Hi! Kevie here!"

I was so surprised he answered, that I babbled out, "You all right?"

"Youse heard I had a fall?" he asked.

"Yeah. Helen phoned—what happened?"

"Well, when I left youse, I stayed with Amanda for a while, and then I headed further north for a week. But the weather turned ugly, so I did a three-point turnaround because I couldn't find the fork in the road—headed back south. It's a long story—I'll tell youse when I see youse. I finally ended up back here in Ballina, and after I arrived, I took a walk through the local park that connects with the RSL club. I was goin' there for somethin' to eat — maybe a schnitzel — when along came this good-lookin' woman walkin' her dog. What a bitch!" he exclaimed.

"The woman or the dog?" I asked.

He laughed. "The woman!" he replied. "She stopped to chat, and then her stupid dog wrapped its lead around my legs. I fell over, and she walked off and left me lyin' there! I couldn't move!"

"Who found you?" I asked.

"An old lady was walkin' by. She noticed I was in trouble, so she asked a young fella to use his mobile phone to call an ambulance. They took me off to emergency, and now I'm wearin' a moon boot!" said Kevin.

"Moon boot? What's that?" I asked.

"It's a big, big boot on my right leg to protect it from any knocks. The doctor says I should be wearin' it for about four weeks," returned my uncle.

"Do you need us to do anything for you?"

"It's all done. Everythin's been taken care of. The RSL club are lettin' me park in their car bay. I'm livin' in the club durin' the day and sleepin' in the van at night," said a now very enthusiastic Kevin, "and I gotta' tell youse—they have the best chicken schnitzel I have tasted anywhere!"

Once I heard his enthusiasm coming through the telephone, particularly relating to his favourite schnitzel, then I knew he would be all right.

"Maybe you should head back here to rest up?" I offered.

"I can't drive with this moon boot on. If it's OK with youse, I'll give youse a call once the boot is off to let youse know I'm all good. Then I'm headin' south to catch up with family, and then maybe back to your place after that."

I responded with, "Sounds good!"

After final pleasantries were exchanged, we both hung up. I called Aunt Helen to let her know her brother was well following a mishap with a dog and a good-looking woman in a park in Ballina.

I heard a sigh of relief coming through the telephone, followed by, "Just like Kevin—always in the thick of it when it comes to women."

#

Many weeks had passed since we had received Helen's worrying telephone call. It was a warm autumn evening, just before twilight time. We were again on our front verandah, peering at our sky slowly turning into black towards the east. Clouds with light grey underbellies were moving slowly across the blue-black canvas, heading toward the bay.

Our immediate atmosphere was pleasant—not too cold, not too hot. It had rained during the morning, but heat from the western sun had dried up most leftover puddles of water. You could still see puffs of steam slowly rising off small haphazard puddles on the black bitumen road.

Again, we were enjoying our usual cold one and a lively chat. Anne commented on my new winter shirt—a woolly combination of red-and-black checks.

"It looks very warm and comfortable", she observed. Apart from my new winter shirt, our subject of the day was our need to celebrate our upcoming 40th wedding anniversary. We both wanted to travel. Maybe go on a road trip, or an ocean cruise. It was difficult to plan given we had our animal menagerie to consider. Our neighbours had offered to take care of our animals for a short time if we decided to travel, but none sounded enthusiastic.

We had decided to go on a short road trip anyway. We would travel down the coast for about a week. Our first stay would be at the casino for several days, then a beach stay, after that. If opportunity presented itself, as it always did in our younger years, we would plan an ocean cruise for later in the year. An ocean cruise to Papua New Guinea was on our mind because we had never been there. We had visited most other parts of the Pacific during our married life, but we have never been to Papua New Guinea.

Our lively chat was interrupted by a van pulling up in front of our house. It parked itself under our golden melaleuca tree. There was no movement from inside. Then our telephone rang. It was just before six o'clock. I jumped up from my usual seat as best I could whilst thinking the caller might be Aunt Helen or Uncle Kevin. I proceeded with haste to the summoning telephone, which rings only eight times before it goes into voice recording mode. I always arrive just as the changeover click is heard.

I'll fix that bloody phone one day, I thought to myself as I returned to the upper front verandah, which was now looking like it needed a good scrub. Anne was watching the stationary van very intently.

"Any movement from the van yet?" I enquired.

"None. I wonder who it is?" Anne replied.

"Maybe it's Kevin, but I can't make out the van type or colour 'cause it's getting dark", I surmised.

Then we heard the customary *clunk* of the van door as it opened, and a familiar elderly man appeared. He was facing away from where we were sitting. With his haphazard movement, he stepped forward, then sideways, and then turned again to face us. One thing that was missing was a shock of collar-length white hair.

"I think it's Kevie!" I concluded with a smile, so then stood up to greet him.

"Finally made it back I see," I shouted.

"Hi Chris and Anne! It's Kevie! I tried to ring youse to let ya know I was comin'—no answer!"

I replied, "No worries. The door's unlocked, you know how to come up."

Kevin proceeded through our front gate and yelled back, "I've got to use the dunny for a toot first!" He made his way through our front entry door, with a look of anguish on his face.

My uncle has some words that he uses which were alien to us at first, like "use the dunny", or toilet, and *toot*, which of course means to have a leak, a wee, a number one. He also uses the word dinner to mean lunch, but we'd become familiar with his vocabulary during his first coming. We speak his language.

The last time we had seen my uncle, he was going to "look up an old address or two", so once he came upstairs and was in a more relaxed state, I asked him how he went with that old address.

He sat down in his usual seat, looked at me, looked at my new winter shirt, then said, "Where's ya axe lumberjack!" With a chuckle he then went on to say, "Amanda? Yeah, I got to her place. Had a great time over the four days I stayed. We went night clubbin' and to the movies. She's still the same—hasn't changed."

Anne and I have never met Amanda, but Kevin has told us much about her. He informed us that he had to leave because Amanda was returning to work on the Wednesday. So he headed further north, but the weather was going crazy. He turned around and headed back south. He was intending to call in to see Amanda on the way through, and possibly stay over for a few more days, but she told him she was having the inside of her house painted. When Kevin said to her he could sleep anywhere, Amanda responded by saying her boyfriend was the painter, and he would be living with her while he painted her house.

My uncle then decided to call in to see us, but realised he had some urgent bills to pay, so he headed south to do some banking. He needed to drive to Newcastle.

"From there, I made the mistake of droppin' into Hunter Street to revisit my youth—the good old sixties. They were fun times," he narrated. "It seems I picked up the worst strain of flu—probably from the people in the pub. The place was packed with people coughin' and sneezin'. I had a chicken schnitzel dinner, but it wasn't much good." He told us that he became very ill a few days later. He thought it may have been the chicken schnitzel causing his sickness. The next day, a passer-by saw him lying in the street gutter beside his van, the worse for wear, so telephoned an ambulance.

He was taken to hospital and admitted to intensive care. He spent three weeks in there and, at times, the doctors and nurses thought he would not survive.

"But you can't keep a fighter down. Not bad for an old fella, survivin' that strain of the flu. It's killed hundreds of young 'uns this year, poor buggers," his narrative supported by his moist eyes.

"Sorry Kevie, we didn't know you were going through that," I replied on behalf of both of us.

"Youse couldna' done nothin' anyway," was Kevin's response to my concern. "I'm just glad youse didn't need to come to my funeral! Then after bein' discharged, I decided to head back here to see youse. I stopped at Ballina along the way for dinner and encountered that bloody dog and its bitch as I was makin' my way to the club. Youse know the outcome to that story!"

Anne commented, "I see you've had a haircut. We didn't recognise you at first. You don't look like a cockatoo any more!"

My uncle laughed; I think because he didn't know how else to respond to Anne's observation.

I changed the subject with, "How long are you planning to stay?"

"Just as long as youse can stand me."

"You know where everything is," I said. "Get yourself freshened up and we'll see you inside for dinner—tea."

"I only eat dinner at noon, and I only eat fruit at night—always have done. Tea comes in a cup," he emphatically replied.

Anne and I looked at each other. We didn't say anything. This was news to us. When my uncle first came, he enjoyed our evening meals.

"No worries," I replied, then invited him to have his smoke while Anne and I headed inside to prepare our dinner.

He came in after his smoke, declared he wasn't feeling well and that he would catch up with us in the morning.

#

The next afternoon, Kevin joined us again on the front verandah for a cool drink and a lively chat.

"All's well?" I asked.

Kevin responded with, "All good. Musta' been a rotten chicken schnitzel I ate at the club yesterday."

Anne looked up from her word puzzle book and replied, "I wouldn't eat at that club. There's been a lot of talk about food poisoning over the last year. I hear the women complaining when I play bingo there."

"Remind me not to eat there no more!" Kevin exclaimed. "Have youse had any problems with vandals in the neighbourhood? I'm just askin' 'cause I heard a report on the radio yesterday when I was recuperatin'—local gangs causing problems in the area."

I thought about that for several moments, and then replied, "I don't think that problem is in this area. It seems to be with youth gangs down south. We don't have that problem here but let me tell you a funny story about vandals in our street—it happened years ago."

"I like your uncle's stories better. You get lost in the story line," was Anne's critical response.

"I don't have any stories to tell youse today, Anne," said Kevin. "I'm still recoverin'.

So come on, let's have it and give me mind a rest for the afternoon!"

I then proceeded to tell my story about our newspaper delivery each Saturday morning.

#

Many years ago, our Saturday morning newspaper was full of general and employment advertisements, together with a weekend magazine, all rolled up together into one very large paper roll, held together by several rubber bands, which was then pitched by the local paper-boy into our front yard.

I was sure that, each Saturday morning, the delivery boy took great delight in attempting to knock over our old freestanding timber letterbox by pitching that very heavy newspaper at it, because I would often find the newspaper on the ground next to a tilted letterbox (which I then had to right each weekend).

In frustration, I said to Anne early one Saturday morning, "I'm going to replace that bloody old letterbox with a new aluminium one so they can't knock it over!"

Anne's response was, "You talk a lot about doing it, but you never do."

So that very day, I did.

The following Saturday morning, I was awoken by the sound of a very heavy rolled up newspaper hitting the new aluminium letterbox. *Boionnnnng* was the loud contact sound reverberating through our neighbourhood. I went to investigate and was pleasantly surprised to see the new letterbox still standing.

"What's your story got to do with vandals?" Kevin enquired.

"Stay with me," I counselled.

Weeks went by. *Boionnnnng* was heard out front at around six o'clock every Saturday morning.

"I'm going to lie in wait and catch that bloody idiot," I said to Anne one Friday night.

"One day, maybe," was Anne's reply.

Come Saturday morning, I slept soundly and didn't rise until around seven o'clock. I went downstairs to pick up the newspaper so I could take it back to bed and read it while sipping my favourite coffee. I was shocked to see the top of our new letterbox lying next to the very heavy, rolled up Saturday morning newspaper.

I went upstairs with the evidence and said to Anne, "He's finally done it!" and presented her with the head of the decapitated letterbox.

"Well, what are you going to do about it?"

"You know I'll take so much, and then I'll do something about it. I'm going down to the newsagent to register our complaint."

I stormed off to the newspaper shop. There was a line of white-haired, grey-haired or no-haired old men, waiting patiently to buy their beloved Saturday morning newspaper. I stormed past all of them and placed the decapitated head of the letterbox on the serving counter. Everyone in the shop stopped and looked.

"What's this?" enquired the lady shop owner, pointing at my letterbox head.

"It's my new letterbox, destroyed by your bloody idiot delivery boy! He pitched your newspaper at our letterbox and knocked the top off! He's broken it!"

The shopkeeper replied with, "You'd better go see my husband. He's outside in the car park."

I stormed off looking for her husband. I was fuming.

For several minutes, I roamed the western car park looking for Paul, the newspaper shop owner. I saw his balding head pop up above the bonnet of his delivery van (a white one, just like Kevin's) so I bounded over.

"Paul! Paul! Look at what your stupid delivery boy has done to our new letterbox. He keeps pitching the heavy Saturday paper at our letterbox—and this is the result!"

Paul was silent. He looked at me, then looked at our decapitated letterbox, and then quietly said, "Our usual delivery boy called in sick, so I had to make the deliveries. I know where your house is, but I can't recall that I hit your letterbox. I would have realised it from the *Boionnnnng* sound it makes."

"Here's the evidence! This was lying next to your newspaper!" I cried.

Paul could see that I was upset, so he offered to pay for the damage.

"I'm not looking for any compensation, I just don't want your boy using our letterbox as a target. It makes a hell of a racket! It's just not acceptable so early in the morning!"

With that off my chest, I stormed off.

"Again, what's this got to do with vandals?" Kevin interrupted. "Stay with me," I pleaded.

I returned home, found Anne, and told her. "I got right up 'em!"

"Good for you," she replied.

I then went to put some tools together and started to work out how to replace the head of the letterbox on its aluminium post, still standing solid in the ground.

Good neighbour Karl was observing what I was doing from his front verandah. He wandered over, to give me a helping hand, I thought.

As he approached, he called out, "I see they did it to yours too!"

I queried, "Who did what to whom?"

Karl pulled up on the street side of our front fence and declared, "Late last night, there were about ten vandals. They went up and down our street screwing off the tops of everyone's letterboxes, yours included. I was sitting on the front verandah having a smoke and watchin' 'em."

At the conclusion of my story, Kevin let out a belly laugh, and then said, "Ya gotta' be very careful when it comes to circumstantial evidence! I learnt that in the union."

These days, I am one of those white-haired, balding old men waiting patiently in line at the newspaper shop to buy my beloved Saturday morning newspaper.

#

The coming days fused into several more weeks. We noticed Kevin was having mood swings once more, but worse than during his first coming. His visit to Amanda and then a three-week stint in hospital seemed to have had some sort of negative effect on him.

Apart from not partaking of any evening meal, he would only have bland cereal with almond oil in the mornings. With breakfast came a very moody Kevin. But the opposite disposition was presented in the afternoons and evenings. The old Kevin was with us once more after noon. Anne again decided not to talk to him in the mornings, because, with her condition, he often upset her.

Following my uncle's return, each morning I would go through the same ritual as before of leaving on the breakfast bar a cup for his coffee, a bowl and spoon for any cereal he might want, and a section of the morning newspaper for him to read. That way he didn't have to talk to us, and we didn't have to talk to him.

One morning he lost it. "This is not the right bloody spoon to use for cereal!" he bellowed, "and I don't read this rag," he waved the newspaper, "so don't leave it on the table!"

I politely responded with, "Oka-a-y!" and thought, *Gee, he must have had a bad night's sleep!*

Another time, he focused on my receding hairline. "You're the only family member I know who's goin' bald," he blurted out.

As time rolled on, the very negative Kevin (or 'Mr Hyde' as we referred to his negative personality) started to creep into the evening period before his smoke. I remember on another occasion, while Anne and I were watching an Australian Rules football match, he came up from downstairs and sat with us.

He looked at the television screen, and then proceeded to accuse all Australian football players of being gay.

"How do you figure that?" I enquired.

"When I was in Melbourne a few years ago, three of 'em came out!" he snapped.

"Yeah, maybe... so what? That doesn't make them all gay," I reasoned. "I know of at least two rugby league players who've come out, but that doesn't make all rugby league players gay, does it?"

Kevin looked away into the distance. What surprised us was that Kevin had stated emphatically that he was intending to vote *Yes* if we ever went to a referendum for legalising gay marriage. Truly he had become an enigma to us at this time. I began to realise my uncle was bigoted.

After a short silence, Kevin changed the course of our conversation, but stayed with the football theme. "When I played for the Pumpkin Pickers, Johnny Sattler from Kurri was in the team. He was an unknown in those days before he went to Sydney. Back in those days, men were men. None of this sissy stuff goin' on like today," he declared.

I wasn't sure what he meant by "sissy stuff", so I engaged him further.

"I'm sure men were men—and still are, and women were women—and still are. And some crossed over to different dressing rooms from time to time, and some stayed there—maybe as far back as when Adam was a boy and Eve was a girl," I teased. "It's just that this century seems to me to be the century of truth, given all this other stuff coming out now, like institutional child abuse and the like," I theorised.

"I just don't like Australian Rules!" Kevin bellowed.

The bigotry started to flow again, so I enquired, "You love your rugby league—what about rugby union?"

Kevin snapped back, "No, union is too close to league. I only watch league."

"That's because you played it Kevie. Anne and I enjoy any football game, it doesn't matter what code. It's good entertainment, and far better that those silly reality shows on the TV these days."

"People watch those stupid reality shows, otherwise the network bosses wouldn't keep dishin' that rubbish up. Anyhow, it's all scripted. It's not reality, only the gullible don't know it!" Kevin snorted back.

At this time, I thought it might be a good idea to change the subject again because he seemed to be having a bad time of it.

"I think it might be time for your evening puff. Go see if it's going to rain," I said as I got up and moved into kitchen to prepare our evening meal.

I turned on the stove to heat up a pan of water. I also turned on our noisy exhaust fan. Kevin didn't move. As I started to prepare the evening meal, I heard him say something, but I didn't know whether it was intended for me or Anne.

Then I heard him clearly yell, "Ya goin' deaf!"

I returned from the kitchen and asked, "What's up?"

"What's up?" Kevin again snorted. "I was talkin' to ya about this segment on the TV about the Prime Minister and you didn't hear me. Ya goin' deaf, an' you're ten years younger than me!" he said indignantly.

"Probably because of the noise from the TV and the range hood over the stove. When I'm cooking there's a lot of noise in the kitchen," I explained. To take his focus away from this new attack, I asked, "What's the Prime Minister up to?"

Kevin was stern in his reply. "Back-stabbin' anyone he can, of course!"

I decided to stay in the kitchen, a place of safety out of harm's way, until our evening meal was cooked, and Kevin had partaken of his smoke. I thought to myself, *He might go to sleep then, and we'll have some peace.*

Anne and I eat our meal in front of the television most nights. Yes, we know this is bad manners, but given Anne's condition, it's much safer for her because she feels comfortable in her modified armchair, not threatened by anything she can't control.

While Kevin was smoking on our front verandah, I set up Anne's TV table. I served up our dinner and sat down to listen to the evening news.

Kevin returned from having his smoke and made his way to his lounge seat located behind mine in the living room. As I began to eat another superbly cooked evening meal, listening to the bickering between all sides of politics on the evening news, Kevin pleaded, "Turn it up, will ya? I can't hear a thing."

That's a bit odd, I thought to myself, *considering he was telling me I was going deaf!*

A segment then came on regarding the royals. I could hear Kevin whispering and mumbling something, so I asked, "What's up, Kevie?"

He grumbled louder so we could both hear, "Bloodsuckin' royals, that's what's up. Ya know they have big investments in palm oil production and a lotta' other industry that's bad for this planet. And they bludge on their people." There was venom in his voice.

"How so?"

"Well, they do nothin' for their people an' get paid millions—trillions," was his curt reply.

Kevin's comments regarding the royals went spinning around in my head, just like our washing machine on rinse cycle. After clearing my throat, I responded with, "I'm not a true-blue supporter one way or the other but seems to me the royals live in a fish bowl. Everyone's prodding, poking, pointing at them, wanting them to make a mistake. They wouldn't have a minute's rest. I wonder if it keeps them awake at night knowing that the damn paparazzi are sneaking around wanting to get an embarrassing picture so they can make money from it. Sorry, but they are the sufferers. They have my support when it comes to needing privacy. In fact, I admire the Queen for her age and what she does in the public eye. She carries herself very professionally. Her father and mother would be very proud." With that, I returned to eat my now cold evening meal.

As I was chowing down, Kevin closed out this part of our conversation with, "Everyone's got a right to an opinion—I bet she was complicit in The Dismissal!"

Not wishing to add any fuel to the now burning fire, I held back on any further comments even though I wanted to know more about The Dismissal.

There was silence for a while, and then a news bulletin came on the television.

"Breaking news! Britain has formalised its proposed departure from the EU in writing to the Secretary General…"

As the announcer presented her news, I asked Kevin, "What do you think about that?"

"Probably a good thing for us," he responded. "The Brits left us flounderin' an' went off to join the union. We recovered by openin' up local Pacific trade. Seems their union hasn't worked for 'em, but it can work for us. New trade in primary industry with the Brits I think — more cows and sheep for the Brits — should be very good for our primary producers."

I was expecting something different from Kevin on this issue, knowing that he dislikes the royals. His opinion of Brexit was refreshing. I also could not understand why the Brits would want to turn their backs on the Commonwealth of Nations in the first place and concentrate only on Europe. My view has always been that more markets available lead to lower prices, and availability of all food types at any time of the year. If some nations suffer from drought, bushfire, floods or pestilence, as we often do, then other markets are able to supply.

"Just to let youse know," piped up Kevin, changing the subject. "I have some news of me own. I think I'm gunna' hit the road again, maybe doin' some house-sittin'."

#

The following afternoon, Anne and I sat on our front verandah. We were being entertained by a flock of rainbow lorikeets bouncing in and out of, and around, the golden melaleuca tree. A gentle breeze came in from the south, keeping things cool. We were enjoying our own company as we sat and waited for my uncle's arrival from his usual day out. We were intending to test him on his house-sitting abilities this very afternoon.

Kevin arrived on time and parked, in his usual way, under our golden melaleuca tree. He then alighted from his van in the usual way and ambled over the terrain. As he made his way through our front door, he yelled out, "I'll be up shortly!"

"OK, Kevin," returned Anne.

It was some time before we heard him coming up our stairs, each of his forward steps taking longer to negotiate than the step before. He arrived at the threshold of our front verandah and enquired, "Gidday! What's happenin'?"

"Same old, same old," I said.

"Any cold ones left?"

"Make yourself comfortable. I'll get you one," I replied as I passed by him and headed for the refrigerator.

"Here you go!" I said as I handed Kevin a very cold can of beer from the freezer compartment.

"Salute," he announced as he sat down.

We returned the "Salute", and then I added, "Tell us about your plans to house-sit."

Kevin continued from his announcement of the day before. He told a story about meeting a lady in a white van many months ago during one of his open road travels.

"She house-sits for a small fee," he said, then went on to explain that when a family wants to go away on a holiday or for business, they call in the 'White Lady'. He was toying with the idea of doing the same as the White Lady but didn't know how to go about it.

I said, "That sounds like a challenge. Have you had any experience with house-sitting before?"

Kevin replied, "None, but youse know me. I can talk me way into any situation—and out of it. Shouldn't be too hard a job!"

"I think it's a bit more than just squatting. The owners might want you to look after their animals. One or two might be aggressive, or even get ill while you're looking after them. You'd have to call a vet, and who pays the bill?"

Kevin looked at me with his cheeky grin. "All good devil's advocate stuff, but ya just can't lie in bed wrapped up in cotton wool." The congenial Kevin was with us that afternoon.

It took us by surprise that my uncle was so positive before his smoke, so I took the opportunity to declare, "Anne and I have been planning a short break this year. We want to head south down the coast and stay where we please."

"How long youse plannin' to be away?" enquired Kevin. "I think around seven days," I said.

Anne had sowed this seed in my mind—to test my uncle's ability to look after someone else's goods and chattels. If my uncle could manage our house for one week, then he should be able to manage several weeks. This would then be an opportunity for Anne and me to go cruising and celebrate our 40th wedding anniversary, just the two of us. If my uncle proved successful in this first trial, we would then feel more comfortable with letting him do the same during our ocean cruise.

I felt it would do Anne and I a lot of good to get away from my uncle for a while. He was starting to play the 'I am your uncle' card, which I was objecting to. He was grinding me down, but I didn't let Anne know this.

That evening in bed, she said to me, "I just had a bad thought. He might burn someone's house down!"

"Gee, I hope he doesn't start with our house!"

#

My uncle jumped at the opportunity. He was very enthusiastic but pointed out to us that he didn't want to be paid.

"Youse have given me a place to stay to find meself again, so no money please. I want to do this for youse."

So for the next week, I explained to Uncle Kevin what needed to be done to manage the house over a seven-day period, which I thought he would write up in a notebook, but he didn't.

I said to Anne late one night, after Kevin had gone to bed, "I've shown Kevin what needs to be done for the week, but he didn't write it down. I don't think a man of his age would have that great a memory."

Anne replied, "Maybe he wrote it down when he went to bed?"

"Yeah, I didn't think of that. Maybe he did—but he hasn't asked for pen or paper."

That night in bed, I was restless. I couldn't sleep thinking that, if some emergency happened while we were travelling, Kevin may not know how to deal with it, or not know who to call. If Snoopy became seriously ill, would Kevin know what to do? I decided to test him the next evening before his smoke.

"Did you write down all of my instructions, Kevie?" I enquired while we sipped cold ones on the front verandah.

"It's all up here!" he replied, pointing to his head.

"Do you know what to do if Snoopy or one of the other animals becomes ill?" I tested.

"I'll give one of ya sons a call if I can't get youse. One of 'em will know what to do," was his confident reply.

I decided to write out all of the instructions and place them on the door of our refrigerator, so that as Kevin passed by, he would notice the post and hopefully read it.

"All good," thanked Kevin when I explained what I was intending to do. "That wouldn't have worked in me younger days. Let me tell youse a story about a young fella who left school too early. He couldn't read nor write, so he had to go back to school as an old fella."

"Aaahhh good," chirped in Anne. "We haven't had one of your stories for a long while."

Chapter 8
Degrees of Separation

Kevin arrived at the trade union school with battered port in hand. It was the same port that, in his youth, he had carried with him around Queensland. He was ready and willing to learn. The first class he attended was an introduction to reading and writing skills.

These skills he needed to master if he were to take on the role of secretary of the union.

Prior to John Maitland agreeing to pay my uncle's way through union school, Maitland wanted to know how Kevin was able to gain, and hold onto, the position of organiser, an important union position that requires good understanding of the written word. Maitland had said to Kevin, "An organiser requires to have readin' and writin' skills to maintain the position, Kevie; how did you manage that for so long?"

Kevin respectfully replied, "Well, I pretended I was readin' a newspaper, or a paper handed to me for readin'. Of course, I could recognise some small words that I would whisper out loud. Then I would stop for a while and ask some simple questions like 'What do ya think about all this?' or 'What course of action do ya think needs takin'?' From the responses, I could put together what was goin' on."

"Very clever, Kevie!" was the union president's observation.

At union school, the course instructor presented an overview of the subject that included an understanding of words, phrases, vowels, phonetics and the reading of newspapers.

At this point, Kevin raised his hand and, once acknowledged by the instructor, stood up and asked, "Why newspapers? Everyone knows ya should only believe a quarter of what ya read in 'em and about half of what ya see in 'em."

The instructor replied, "A very good observation you make, Kevin — sorry — Kevie.

"It's all about understanding the news of the day, particularly the political content. You need to master the unique words and phrases used in the political arena. Journos have a propensity to bend the truth to suit their needs to sell their story, so the common phrase 'read between the lines' means exactly what you have raised."

My uncle settled into union school. His positive outlook ingratiated him with all of the other students and the instructors. He always had a joke, a story to tell and a readiness to help those around him. He possessed a high-quality, high-quantity work ethic.

During his time at union school, Kevin was curious to know the origin of it, and the reason why it was named after Clyde Cameron, a Minister in the Whitlam Government. As his knowledge of reading and writing improved, he was often found sitting in the library researching many subjects of interest to him. He had a big thirst for knowledge.

Kevin researched Clyde Cameron. He found out that Cameron was the son of a shearer of Scottish descent. Cameron left school at fourteen to work as a shearer. During the very worst years of the Great Depression, he was unemployed, and the experience of joblessness was one that he would never forget, so he always championed workers' rights. Cameron was very active in the Workers Union. He became an organiser and progressed to state president. Eventually he was elected to federal parliament.

Cameron proved to be an intelligent and able parliamentarian. When the Whitlam Government came to power, Cameron was promoted to Minister for Labour.

How very appropriate, Kevin thought. He developed an empathy with the essence of Clyde Cameron because they both left school at an early age, were both basically illiterate when young, and both lived for their union. Kevin learnt that Cameron was instrumental in improving the pay and conditions of public servants by using the public sector to set new workers' benchmarks, which he hoped would be extended to the private sector. In time, the private sector matched the public servant wage level, because the private sector was finding it difficult to employ skilled labour.

Cameron supported the feminist movement. He hired Mary Gaudron (the first woman on the High Court bench) to argue before the Arbitration Commission for equal pay for women workers. Kevin looked to Clyde Cameron as a role model.

Kevin then researched the history of the Clyde Cameron Trade Union Academy. He discovered the Whitlam Government had a primary objective of modernising the labour movement through education of its workers. A workers' university was one of their dreams. The Whitlam Government believed that education was the key to workers' success. Educating workers would quell their frustration at not being able to get anywhere, thus improving their work and home life through increased wages, leading to increased self-worth. If any worker wanted to learn, then their respective union would nominate them for a training position at the school.

The creation of the workers' school was also intended to better educate the worker to resist exploitation. This would be achieved through improved reading and writing skills. At that time, like Kevin, many workers around the country were illiterate or semi-literate.

"So I did me time and graduated, not only from the college, but also to the secretary's position," said a very proud Kevin, one cold winter's afternoon. "I enjoyed this new position very much. There was a lotta' travellin' involved, and some very unpleasant stuff to handle, but it was one of the best times of me life."

"What sort of unpleasant stuff?" Anne enquired.

"I can remember one time — it still gives me grief at times — I was at one of the coal mines doin' union business with the bosses when we were all alerted to an accident underground. One of the workers got caught in a hopper and was crushed to death," Kevin sadly announced.

"That would have been hard to take," I consoled.

"Yeah, it was. Sometimes I still have nightmares 'bout it. I had the unpleasant duty of informin' his family. I had to knock on his front door. I can still see his wife in my mind's eye when I told her. I've never seen anyone so distressed. It was just so very sad," he forcefully mumbled.

Kevin went on to explain to us how the union went about taking over responsibility for workers' safety, not trusting the employers on this issue due to their poor historical record.

"Of course, safety today — not just workers' safety — is enshrined in legislation to protect everyone. There's even *safety in design* legislation to make sure design is as safe as it can be when the construction is complete."

I decided to change the course of our discussion, which I felt was becoming morbid, so I asked, "Why was the school named after Clyde Cameron?"

Kevin looked a little bit puzzled. "I don't know. Never found that out officially. You'd think there would've been somethin' in the library 'bout it. I think it was because he was Minister for Labour at the time of construction, or somethin' like that. Cameron was a modest man."

Then Kevin suddenly changed his thought track with, "Do youse know about the six degrees of separation?"

"Someone who knows someone, who knows someone, who knows someone, who knows someone, who then knows someone who knows the Queen or the Pope, or something like that?"

"Spot on! I can tell youse I was there when they sacked Whitlam. I was there when Joh Bjelke-Petersen decided he was good enough to become prime minister of this country. I was there when Nelson Mandela addressed the Workers Union, and I was there for Gough and Margaret Whitlam's' trail-blazin' *Light on the Hill* lecture. None of that, six degrees of separation stuff—it was first degree for me!"

"I heard about 'The Dismissal'. Was that the sacking of Whitlam?" asked Anne.

"In a nutshell," responded Kevin, "it was all about revenge politics. The conservatives were dirty because they lost government after somethin' like twenty years. They sided with the Governor-General to get rid of the Labour government. They blocked supply so the government couldn't pay its way. Labour and Liberal have hated each other's guts since that day. Each party strives to humiliate the other. A lotta' two-faced back-stabbin goin' on all the time. No wonder we're the laughing stock of the world!"

Kevin went on to explain his understanding of the history of 'The Dismissal'. "When the Whitlam Government came to power, they had a nine-seat majority. They set about modernising a large number of government policies, drafted and offered new legislation, and the Clyde Cameron College was one of their initiatives. They sought to improve public facilities, but the public itself didn't like the rapid change, nor did the conservatives.

"The Whitlam Government never had a majority in the senate. The conservatives had a one-seat majority.

"I guess that's what the people wanted in case the incomin' government proved to be a dud. The balance of power further shifted towards the conservatives because of the bloody-mindedness of one Sir Joh Bjelke-Petersen, the Premier of Queensland—I refer to him as 'Sergio'. He nominated an inexperienced Labour politician to fill a vacancy in the senate. Said politician was shunned by his own party members, so he sided with the conservatives, resulting in the balance of power shiftin' further to them. When it came down to approvin' House of Representatives legislation, the conservatives blocked it in the senate all the time. The liberal-controlled opposition blocked supply in the senate after Sergio's manipulations, which forced the Governor-General to take action. He thought the only way forward was to sack the Whitlam Government, so he did. News of the sacking spread all over the country that afternoon like a rat up a drainpipe, triggerin' immediate protest demonstrations. I was there the day after. I was on the steps of Parliament House when the official response from the Queen's representative was read out by the town crier. I was there to organise union demonstrations, and I was disgusted by the Queen's response. I remember her rep's reply almost word for word to this day. It was Pontius Pilate stuff."

Kevin was getting increasingly agitated. "'On behalf of the Queen', her representative read out to the crowd, 'as we understand the situation here, the Australian Constitution firmly places the prerogative powers of the Crown in the hands of the Governor-General as the representative of the Queen of Australia. The only person competent to commission an Australian Prime Minister is the Governor-General, and the Queen has no part in the decisions which the Governor-General must take in accordance with the Constitution. Her Majesty, as Queen of Australia, is watching events in Canberra with close interest and attention, but it would not be proper for her to intervene in person in matters which are so clearly placed within the jurisdiction of the Governor-General by the

Constitution Act'."

Kevin concluded, "What a cop-out! I think she was complicit! So we all went back to the polls after much national protestin' and agitation. Labour lost the fresh election because of the public's fear of more change and the demonising of labour by the conservatives."

"Interesting times in politics," I observed.

"They were," responded Kevin, "but there was more. After the nation settled down and wounds started to scab over, we all went back to our routines. Then about decade later, Sergio decided he wanted to become prime minister of this country."

My uncle went on to tell us how Sir Joh Bjelke-Petersen (Kevin's 'Sergio') believed he was the saviour of the country at that time, so decided to rally for the Prime Minister's position. Sir Joh made his intention to run by generating a flurry of media activity. "Feeding the chooks" was Sir Joh's reference to the snippets he would feed a news-hungry press, but only those journalists he could trust.

It was speculated that Sir Joh could run for a federal seat in Queensland, win that seat and then move to the federal level of politics, where he would then be automatically anointed prime minister.

The leader of the Federal Liberal Party, now back in opposition, was recorded as saying that Sir Joh was "strong on incentive but short on reality". The incumbent Prime Minister of the time, Bob Hawke, could barely contain his delight at the conservative infighting between states, particularly Queensland versus the Federal Liberal Party, so a potential challenge from Sir Joh was very welcomed.

An irony of Sir Joh's run for federal office was that his appeal had always rested on his claim to represent Queensland's best interests in the face of a hostile federal political system. His pro-Queensland and anti-Commonwealth "federal bashing" approach was inconsistent with his push to become the prime minister of the Commonwealth. "I guess he wanted to rename the whole country 'Queensland'," exclaimed Kevin.

Regardless of the challenges Sir Joh faced, he remained outspoken about his chances of becoming prime minister, declaring that nobody else in Australian politics possessed "my experience in politics, my policies for this country, and my determination to make them work".

So the Joh for PM roadshow commenced. It started off in Brisbane and rolled out towards the national capital, passing through as many cities and towns as they could visit, with Sir Joh warning that the conservatives could not possibly win government in the upcoming election, even though he was a conservative himself. Sir Joh was trying to establish himself as the "popular alternative" to the then Federal Liberal leader.

As the Joh for PM roadshow crossed state borders, it moved from town to town, leaving puzzled people in its wake. Workers would be there to heckle and jeer Sir Joh at these hastily organised rallies. After several weeks on the road, the Joh for PM rally arrived in Newcastle, where the Workers Union was waiting. A large crowd of workers arrived for Sir Joh's first public address. It was a bitterly cold winter morning, but they still came in droves.

Sir Joh expounded on the virtues of his ability to wrest national politics back into the hands of the conservatives.

At hearing this, Kevin stood up and said, "Sergio, why Joh for PM?"

Sir Joh looked at Kevin and said, "You can't sit on a fence — a barbed wire fence at that — and have one ear to the ground, or you do what I'm doing right now!"

"But Sergio, how do ya plan to boot out the current government?" queried Kevin.

Sir Joh responded, "Well don't you worry about that. You don't tell the frogs anything, before you drain the swamp, and there are more ways of killing a cat than drowning it. Different occasions warrant different methods of annihilating a socialist government."

Kevin came back at him. "Sergio, you always talk in ways we can't understand. You said it yerself in response to a Queensland journo's question last week about mobile phones, so how are we gunna' understand ya when you get in power?"

Sir Joh countered him. "The greatest thing that could happen in Queensland and the nation is if we get rid of all the media. Then we could live in peace and tranquillity."

There was much laughter in the crowd, accompanied by much confusion during this exchange. Some liked what Sir Joh didn't have to say; others were furious; some found him entertaining. After question time was over, Sir Joh and Co packed up and headed onwards, towards the nation's capital.

Kevin finished off this part of his narrative with, "The wheels fell off Sergio's campaign before he reached the capital. No one could understand what he was sayin' outside Queensland!"

"You mentioned you met Mandela; said he shook your hand?" I prompted.

"Sure did," replied Kevin. "I was there when Nelson Mandela addressed the Workers Union when he got outta gaol."

Kevin told us his story about Nelson Mandela. Eight months after Mandela was released from South African prison, and three-and-a-half years before he would be elected his country's president, Mandela went on an international tour to thank all those people whose pressure finally led to his release from prison. The unions had been among the most vocal of supporters, and now Mandela had come to thank those who strongly supported his release.

My uncle was chosen by union management at the Newcastle address to introduce Mandela to the workers because of Kevin's exceptional oratory skills. Kevin cannot remember to this day what he said to the large crowd when introducing Mandela, but he remembers every word Mandela said to him after making his way up the stairs towards Kevin, who was waiting for him on the dais.

After Mandela reached the top of the stairs, he stood on the dais facing the crowd of workers, then offered his right hand to Kevin and said, "I want you to know, Kevin, I want every one of you here today to know that I am here today at this time because of each one of you."

Kevin does remember responding with, "Kevie — everyone calls me Kevie — please call me Kevie!" He didn't know what else to say; he was overawed by the occasion.

Kevin also remembers Mandela's style of speech delivery. "I remember what appeared to me to be his deliberately haltin' delivery of his words. I first thought he might be havin' trouble breathin' after mountin' all them steps, but then I realised it was a deliberate posture he must have learnt to do in gaol. I can remember most of his words. He said:

I can recall how we prisoners of apartheid whispered to each other about your very healthy and militant actions— about your disavowal of an all-white Springbok team from a country where your black brothers and sisters toiled under apartheid rule. Your actions, and those of anti-apartheid workers worldwide, gave us strength and confidence that our just cause would prevail in the end. Today I stand before you happy at the opportunity to thank you in person. Whether we have won the fight or not is irrelevant. The message that we have been able to put across to our people is that it is victory if a man or woman has done his duty on Earth.

Many of our people have accepted the principle and they are prepared to fight back if the government does not want to cooperate with us—and the only way of cooperating with us is to allow people to enjoy the principle of one person, one vote. This is the only way we can establish a non-racial, democratic, united and non-sexist state in South Africa. You all have given us a note of inspiration. You have given us the ability to continue the fight and to continue with the negotiations in the certainty that the world generally, and the people of your great nation, are solidly behind us. I salute you!

"Did youse know Mandela was a big supporter of the feminist movement? His speech writer was a woman at that time he came out here," added Kevin. He then went on with his narrative of the afternoon.

"I also had the very great pleasure of shakin' another famous person's hand in the first degree. I had the duty of introducin' Gough and Margaret Whitlam when Gough delivered his *Light on the Hill* address at Bathurst", said a beaming Kevin. "Gough and Margaret both walked into the dinner party to a standin' ovation. As I was introducin' 'em, the place erupted into cheerin' and applause. Ya couldn't hear yerself think. These two didn't need any introducin'. As they walked up — giants of literature and of stature— they both shook my hand and said, 'Thank you, very kind words', after I introduced 'em. I don't remember what I said. It was a spurof-the-moment thing. I was in awe, but I still remember Gough's very firm handshake, and then he moved on," said a very proud Kevin.

"What was the Light on the Hill address all about?" I asked.

"It was all about thankin' the workers for their labour. It was started by Prime Minister Chifley after the war ended," said Kevin. "Gough was a large man with a large personality. He had a brilliant mind. He could speak about any subject at a moment's notice, and with authority. He was certainly one of the most colourful politicians of our time," he concluded.

Kevin went on to tell his story about this Light on the Hill event. The banquet hall was overflowing with admirers. Gough moved slowly through the room responding to each and every one of them. The audience was totally enthralled. It was a long night.

"Gough was a true statesman. He saw what needed to be done for his country, so he went about organisin' its delivery—not like the self-centred, egotistical pollies of today. Gough is well known for pulling us out of Vietnam. He abolished conscription, reduced the votin' age and drinkin' age to eighteen. He recognised China before the Yanks did. He gave us Medibank, championed equal pay for women, sewered Sydney, removed the death penalty, created free university education and recognised our First Nations peoples in legislation." My uncle rambled on as he counted on his fingers.

"Bet youse didn't know he banned overseas songs for two years so local artists could record those popular overseas songs. This lifted their professional level so we could then compete with overseas artists. Olivia Newton-John is a good example. Gough championed a supporting mother's benefit and a welfare payment system for homeless people. He set up the Legal Office and Law Reform Commission. He introduced needs fundin' for schools, got rid of the British awards system in favour of local national wards... I could go on," he said enthusiastically.

This afternoon's discussion was a very lively and informative one. Anne and I enjoyed it immensely (we think that maybe the extra cold ones consumed that afternoon may have contributed to our receptiveness). I said to Kevin that I knew very little about our country's early politics and the unions. I was very wary of unions because of my first-hand awful experiences.

"Seems to me, Kevie, from what you've been saying, unions were well behaved back in those good old days," I teased.

"More than well behaved," replied Kevin, sensing the tease. "We always abided by the instructions dished out by the Conciliation and Arbitration Commission—an organisation respected by the unions at least, but the bosses didn't if it didn't go their way," he concluded.

"So this Commission was a referee?" I asked.

"Yep, as the title suggests. Conciliation first, then if that failed, off to court."

"I wish that was around in my day. Maybe I would not have had a busted office door," I chuckled.

Kevin looked east for several moments, then turned to me and said, "Unions these days are too militant. They don't need to be like that. Workers today have it good. They are educated; they have a reasonable income for the time they put in compared to my time. There is just no need for militancy. There are still systems in place to resolve disputes without threatenin' to ram a mobile phone down someone's throat—that's thuggery."

I had to agree unconditionally with my uncle's comments. He then went on to tell us about his court skills. "I can tell youse I loved the court work. I used to get very involved in the debate once I knew how to bend the court rules. Loved it! There were several times, after a court case, I was approached by the bosses' reps, who congratulated me on me court work and asked if I'd be interested in workin' for them. Not bad for an illiterate bloke! Then one time I was offered a bribe," said Kevin.

I was curious to know why he had a grin on his face over what would be a criminal offence in those days, and still is today.

"That's pretty serious stuff, Kevie. You could go to gaol over that," I lectured.

"You're right, very serious stuff. So at the next court hearing, I got up and said, 'Your Honour, I am curious to know what the court rules are relatin' to extraordinary payments to unions?'" Kevin added that he was playing dumb in court. He knew very well the rules did not permit ex-gratia payments.

The judge enquired of the nature of the payment, to which Kevin answered, "Your honour, after yesterday's hearing, the employer's rep approached me and offered me personally a large sum of money if I were to withdraw the conditions part of our claim. If I did then they implied they would honour the pay claim."

"Counsel are you accusing the employer's representative of initiating a bribe?" asked the judge, to which Kevin responded, "Oh no, Your Honour. I was simply wantin' to know if out-of-court settlements can be made without the knowledge of the court."

The judge then looked Kevin up and down, and said, "I think you know the answer to that one Counsel, but just in case you do not, remember your training. No out-of-court settlement can be made without the prior knowledge and consent of the court."

"I thought that was the case," replied Kevin. "I request this be mentioned in the court transcript, and I respond to the employer in this court at this time by reaffirming our claim for increased pay and better working conditions, as already lodged with the court, without alteration."

Kevin went on to tell us the employer's representative approached him after the hearing and said, "Well, well. This is the first time I have ever come across an honest union rep."

Kevin was insulted but kept his temper under control. He responded with, "Better luck next time," and then added, "I want you to know we're all honest, hard-workin' people."

The employer's representative walked away, then turned to face Kevin from some distance away and yelled out, "Really? Go check your bosses' bank accounts!"

Kevin stood still. He was in shock. He was having difficulty processing this accusation. Did he mean John Maitland was crooked? Why would he make such an accusation unless he knew something didn't sit right?

Chapter 9
Post Union

Kevin thought that such an accusation of corruption against a man whom he looked up to and would follow anywhere, despite being made by such a well-respected member of the judicial system, was absurd. Kevin admired and respected John Maitland. Kevin had been handpicked by Maitland for the secretary's role. When Maitland realised Kevin was illiterate, he'd organised to send him off to union school. Maitland had a lot of faith in Kevie, and my uncle was a better man for it. Kevin didn't feel obligated to Maitland though. He thought of Maitland as a father figure. Maitland was Kevin's role model, filed in the same file as Clyde Cameron.

Kevin dismissed the accusation as one from a pack of sore losers, but the accusation kept on niggling at him. He began to notice things within the union that were not quite right. Suspicion started to eat away at him. His performance on behalf of the union declined. His soul was not in it. Kevin decided, after many weeks of worry, that he would completely dismiss the accusation. He would put it out of his mind. After all, he was just the union secretary. His role was to do union bidding. His role was not to question its management.

Then came little hints from outside the union walls — from the media and from within the court system — that something was amiss. Proverbial finger-pointing at union management, together with whispers turning into crescendos, caused Kevin more discomfort and more worry.

My uncle did feel, at that time, that it was unreasonable for anyone to accuse John Maitland of corruption. Maitland was a union shining light. He had a big influence in the labour movement, particularly around the Queensland coalfields. Kevin remembered first meeting Maitland at one of these coalfields when Maitland was the district mining union secretary at that time. At their first meeting, Kevin impressed Maitland with his zeal for life and the gift of the gab. Maitland felt that Kevin was much like himself. With assistance from Maitland, Kevin gained a position in one of the Ipswich mines, and so my uncle was employed for a short while, but he didn't like the dirty work underground. My uncle always wanted to be in the sunshine; to meet people from all walks of life. The dirty work was depressing him, so he decided to move on to Brisbane.

Sometime after that, Maitland became national president of the Miners' Union. This new important position within the union required that he move to Sydney. Kevin met Maitland for the second time on the construction site in the Hunter Valley.

Several years later, as Kevin was starting to make his way up the union ladder, so too was Maitland, who become president of the International Federation of Chemical, Energy, Mine and General Workers' Unions, which was based in Europe.

Maitland retired from the union in 2006. He was recognised for his work in mine health and safety and awarded the nation's highest honour. In his retirement, Maitland was again accused of being corrupt. It was determined by a court in 2017 that Maitland had colluded with a government minister to profit from the sale of a mine in 2008, although the conviction was subsequently overturned on appeal. Many of Maitland's supporters were not fully aware of Maitland's financial stake in the mine, nor his plans to on-sell the mine for a profit. The government minister for minerals at that time, dubbed *Sir Lunchalot* because of his propensity to organise long lunchtime meetings, was also found guilty by the same court.

Years before these allegations were ever tested in a courtroom, Kevin decided he'd had enough of working within a corrupt union system, even if the accusations were unsubstantiated at that time (such is the power of the press). He resigned his position from the union. This final decision caused him much grief. I suspect this is when he developed his acute hatred for the word *Maitland*. But this sudden change in life gave him back more family time. He soon realised that things were not the same at home since he had devoted his life to union business.

#

The first few months of being at home full-time were good times for Kevin. He landed a job working for a pest control company, with possibilities of climbing their corporate ladder. As time went by, he began to notice his relationship with his wife, at times, was becoming strained. Usually at sundown, when a husband and wife should come together to talk about their day, Annette would spend this precious time chatting with their daughters. Kevin felt he was being left out of the family.

Kevin's children were growing up fast and they had developed their own agendas. They were no longer the little children who could be easily guided, or persuaded, or smacked if naughty. They had their own minds and they exercised them often.

This feeling of being left out caused Kevin to stay away from home at every opportunity, using it as an excuse not to come home. He was becoming lonely. When he was out of town on assignment, which was quite often, he would stay overnight because he felt there was no reason for him to go home. At times, his wife Annette would accuse him of having an affair because of this behaviour.

By the time Kevin and Annette reached a moment in their relationship where each wouldn't go out of their way for the other, Kevin was spending most nights away from the family home. He came to the realisation that divorce was inevitable.

Of his three children, Kevin worried most about his son Steven, the youngest of the siblings. By the time Steven had reached his teenage years, he still could not grasp the "three Rs" of basic learning: reading, writing and arithmetic. Like Kevin at the same age, Steven was illiterate. If divorce became the only option, then Kevin felt that somehow, he would have to stay in touch with his children, especially Steven, to help them through life.

#

Several years after Kevin resigned his union position, he instigated divorce proceedings because he could not stay any longer in a loveless marriage. The children were devastated. They didn't know their parents were having any problems, particularly the two daughters. Even today, I think they wish their parents were back together again.

Kevin moved into a rental house, with Lake Macquarie at his doorstep. This location served Kevin well. He would be near his children and well away from Maitland, that place he hated most. Lake Macquarie suited him because he could regularly go fishing, which he loved. He bought himself a small boat. He would often reminisce of the many times he spent fishing on the shores of the Hunter River with his older brothers, and sometimes with his father, as he lay back in his small dingy enjoying the peace and serenity whilst floating on his lake of tranquillity.

This time in my uncle's life would prove to be very productive. He was no stranger to hard work. He climbed the corporate ladder of the pest-control business. In return, his salary increased to the point where he decided to look for a mobile home to live in, so he didn't have to pay for the property of others with his hard-earned money.

Kevin's love of the open road led him to buy a large mobile home. This gave him the advantage of owning his own home and doing the thing he loves next best to fishing: driving. And so the legend of Kevie — the man in the van — was born (but that's another story).

Kevin loved to drive. He would drive anywhere, at any time, for his new employer. I remember when we were living in Bondi, Kevin called in several times, unannounced, to see us. He was footloose and fancy-free. He would often stay for dinner, which had my mother scurrying around the kitchen to put something on the table while he and my father would go to the Bondi Royal Hotel for a few *quick ones*.

It was during one of their visits to the Bondi Royal Hotel that they encountered the plainclothes detectives. They were involved in a physical confrontation with the police, and ended up being accommodated overnight, enjoying the hospitality of the Bondi Police, much to my mother's disgust—not because she derided their behaviour, but because she had gone to so much trouble to put a *baked* dinner on the table for them.

During this part of his nomadic life, we all noticed that Kevin no longer showed symptoms of St Vitus' Dance. He could walk straight without his left leg uncontrollably kicking out. No longer did the left side of his face, at times, twitch uncontrollably. Kevin thought that he had "probably grown out of the dance", but since Anne was diagnosed with Parkinson's disease, I wondered about a common connection between these two neurological disorders of the brain, so I researched.

I found out from reading various scientific and medical journals that there is a direct link between being continually exposed to pesticides and insecticides, and the development of neurological disorders in the human brain, such as Parkinson's disease and motor neuron disease.

I formed the view that the pesticides that Kevin and Steven were spraying around back in those days — before safety was a high priority — may have pushed St Vitus into the background as Kevin inhaled the pesticides, but the foreign chemicals now in his body were killing off his neuron production. I think the end result was the development of motor neuron disease. Kevin did not realise that, for the many years he worked in the pest control industry, he had something contrary going on inside his body.

He travelled for a long time, both for business and to feed his wanderlust, but his mind kept him focused on Steven. He worried that Steven did not have the same *out there* personality as he did, so Steven might not make it through life as well as he should.

When Kevin was travelling down the Newell Highway one cold winter morning, looking for that proverbial fork in the road, he saw a sign which stated, *It's Bindi Time! Contact Sewell & Sons for removal.*

For Kevin, that was a Eureka moment. That sign started Kevin thinking about a new road to discovery—a business of his own. He could start up a local business operating throughout the Hunter Valley, with what was left of his savings and the money he would receive from resigning his current pest-control company position. After all, the Hunter Valley was always full of nuisance bindi burrs during wintertime. He would employ Steven to assure both their futures. Kevin could be there for Steven. So Kevin turned his large mobile home around and headed back to the place he despised most yet was always unwillingly drawn back to: *Maitland*.

Several weeks after arriving back, *Mister Bindi Man* burst into existence. Kevin was the mouthpiece. Steven and Kevin were the applicators. Kevin showed Steven what to do and how to do it. Eventually Steven's wife, Annette, would join this weed-eradication company to keep the books in order.

As time went by, Kevin noticed he was not as agile as he should be. His legs were not moving the way he wanted them to, so he would do less and less physical work and more and more office work, such as knocking on doors and booking the spraying jobs.

Eventually Kevin would leave all of the physical work to Steven.

Mister Bindi Man proved to be a very successful business venture. It brought Kevin and Steven closer together. It paid good wages, and it wasn't hard labour. When it wasn't bindi season, they would have regular work spraying to prevent cockroach, ant, rat and mouse infestations.

Steven was the younger version of Kevin. They looked the same, they spoke with the same drawl, and up until Kevin started to suffer the effects of motor neuron disease, they walked the same. It was often a surprise for new clients to see Kevin and Steven together. There was no mistaking they were father and son. Some thought they were brothers.

During the height of success of *Mister Bindi Man*, Kevin met Julie. She was to be his second wife. From the time they first met there was much synergy between them. I remember meeting Julie for the first time at Aunt Helen's place. We were all sitting around in her garage, having a drink and a chat, when Kevin and Julie arrived.

Julie was tall and blonde and a little reserved, which created a little bit of a mystery about her. Kevin and Julie sat together and held hands for the duration of their stay. It was good to see two people sharing the moment. They were in love.

Kevin and Julie eventually married. They were well into their marriage before Kevin realised Julie had *baggage*. She was addicted to alcohol.

"It wasn't there when we was first goin' out," said Kevin, as we chatted on our verandah one fine afternoon, sharing a cold one. "Maybe I was blind to her drinkin' — I don't know — but it soon became a big problem between us. All I could do was be there for her."

"What caused Julie's passing?" I asked cautiously, not knowing how Kevin would react.

"She died from alcoholism a few years ago," Kevin said, trying to remain composed. "It was very sad. It happened so quick—a big shock to us all. Julie's family couldn't believe it. They accused me of not lookin' after her properly."

#

Kevin's increasing lack of balance had worried him. He finally made an appointment to see a doctor, who referred him to a neurologist. The neurologist explained to Kevin that his central nervous system was altering from normal condition to irregularity.

Messages generated by his thoughts were not all reaching his physical body. His motor neurons, the messengers carrying his thoughts, were being killed off before they had a chance to deliver the message. There is no cure for such a degenerative condition. The neurologist predicted a life span for Kevin of five years or less, so Kevin should get his affairs in order.

At first, this life-altering diagnosis was devastating for Kevin, but the negativity that comes with such news didn't last long with him. He decided to change his role within

Mister Bindi Man. He promoted Steven to owner/manager. He stayed on looking after sales by telephone. There was no more knocking on doors for him now that he had problems with accessibility, and now that his physical fits were finally determined—he was suffering from another medical condition.

Kevin didn't hide his affliction. It was a bit hard to, given that it was obvious.

Kevin is a proud man, so he refused to use a walking stick when it was prescribed by his doctor (it was only years later that he relented and used one). I remember one visit, many years ago, when Kevin came to our elder son, Ben's wedding. He would literally lean on me for assistance, or on his sister Helen.

Kevin decided he needed to travel more, to get back on the open road again to see parts of the country he had never been to before, to meet people he believed he had a destiny to meet. He handed over business sales to Steven's wife and replaced his large mobile home with a smaller white van.

"I couldn't manoeuvre the big mobile home no more, so I got this white van and fitted it out with all the necessaries," Kevin had told us when he first arrived. He went back on the road for an extended journey, which saw him travel from one coast to another. Kevie and his travels in his white van added to the Kevie legend. Someone you knew would know of Kevie — *the man in the van* — or they would know someone who knew Kevie. He became larger than life—a living legend. During his travels, he would discuss his affliction with many ordinary people.

"A good subject to start a conversation," he would often say.

During these discussions with ordinary folk, Kevin became convinced that the use of marijuana would help him manage his affliction, so he headed back to test his idea with his neurologist. The neurologist conceded there was evidence, albeit anecdotal, that marijuana showed some benefit for people suffering from neurological disorders, but he could not prescribe its use because he may be committing professional suicide. The Medical Board would take away his licence to practise.

#

I remember when I reached adulthood, I would often wonder about the use of that word *practise* when it came to healthcare professionals. It seemed to me that doctors would keep *practising* on you, as if they never got it right in the first place. Kevin and I had a discussion about this very subject one afternoon on our upper front verandah. I had been very sick as a child, so my mother and I would often visit a medical practice to see a doctor. Of course, Kevin had his afflictions to manage, so he would often have to do the same.

"If ya open up a telephone book at any time, have a look at the list of doctors' names," said Kevin during one afternoon discussion. "You'll find names like Dung or Dungling or Dunglingson, who are specialists in lookin' after ya back passage. Then there's a list of Dr Slaughters—you'd stay away from those ones, wouldn't ya?" he exclaimed with his classic grin.

An interesting observation, I thought. *People working in positions having a family name that states what they do. I remembered working with an acoustic engineer; his job specification was reducing noise. Rumbling type noise was his speciality. His name was Ron Rumble. And then there was policeman called Constable; Breuer who works in a boutique brewery; and Baker who works in a cake shop.*

#

During his visit with his neurologist, Kevin asked if there was any drug he could take, prescribed or otherwise, to reduce his symptoms. His neurologist relaxed and suggested he experiment with marijuana, as suggested by the *roadies*, to understand if it would be of any benefit to him. The neurologist committed to monitoring my uncle's condition over a twelve-month period.

This period yielded positive results for Kevin. He felt more in control of his affliction.

His neurologist decided to extend the monitoring period with a view to publishing the results in a medical journal.

The neurologist could not and would not prescribe marijuana back in those days, so Kevin had to source a supply, "which wasn't hard to do—it's everywhere!" he exclaimed during one of our many discussions concerning his affliction.

So once Kevin started his evening smoke, his affliction became static. It didn't progress. He also found it had another benefit. It stopped his mind racing. It calmed him down. Kevin now has lived three times longer than his first life expectancy prognosis. He is much happier because of it (but only in the afternoons, as we have found out).

My uncle's neurologist did write that medical research paper and presented it to a journal for publication, but they refused to publish it on the grounds that marijuana was, in those days, a prohibited substance. The neurologist was accused of recklessness, so he withdrew his paper, fearing he would lose his licence to practise.

After this episode in his life, Kevin often caught himself thinking about retirement.

Chapter 10
The Eviction

Kevin and Steven stopped work early one windy Friday afternoon because the bindi spray they were using was difficult to control. At times, the weed spray had drenched them due to unpredictable wind gusts. They headed for the local pub for some well-earned refreshment before going home.

As they sat enjoying the first cold one, Steven said to his father, "You're getting' old, old fella. Have you bin thinkin' 'bout retirement, Kevie?"

Kevin had been thinking a lot about retiring, but he did not want to alarm Steven, knowing that Steven relied on him for so much.

He replied, "Well, Steve, I can't do half the work I used to, but if I retire, I'll have to get out of the dump I'm livin' in. I'll probably go back on the open road unless someone makes me an offer I can't refuse."

"I've bin thinkin' about it a lot lately," said Steven. "I need ya close so I kin lean on ya for advice about the business. Annette can keep doin' the bookin's and look after the books, and I'll probably get an apprentice to help me. So don't worry too much. If you want to retire, then go for it, Kevie," Steven counselled.

Kevin would not have any of his children call him 'Dad'. He wanted his children to call him Kevie. I could see the relationship between Kevin and Steven was more on the level of best friends rather than father and son, but my view is that this approach by Kevin ultimately led to the relationship breakdown with Steven. If Steven had respected his father, he would not have done what he did.

Retirement was not discussed again until several months later, when Kevin decided he had had enough after a fall while trying to lift a container of spray. He suffered several bruises and a small cut which he washed continuously with hot water, then treated with antiseptic, not knowing what effect weed spray might have on an open wound.

As Kevin was in bed recovering, Steven called in to "make sure he was still breathing". They conversed for several hours, and then they came to an agreement that would allow Kevin to build his retirement home on Steven and Annette's property at Bishops Bridge. Steven would purchase the Mister Bindi Man business by paying monthly instalments direct to Kevin, which would be his father's retirement pension, and Kevin would then make himself available any time in relation to the business.

For Kevin, this deal sounded like the ideal retirement plan. There was no need to get lawyers in, because, after all, he was dealing with his own son. *What could go wrong?* he thought as they shook hands.

#

Kevin planned a "no steps", two-bed cottage, with plenty of clear space for him to manoeuvre. Viewed from the front of the cottage, there would be a centrally located, wide front door, which would open into the living room. Off each side of the living room would be a bedroom (two in case of a visitor sleepover). At the rear of the living room would be a long bench top that would lead you to the stove top and refrigerator immediately to the left. To the right would be the food pantry. There would be a wide front verandah and a smaller rear verandah. The rear verandah would house the smallest room in the house, the toilet. In essence, Kevin's retirement home would resemble a miniature The Odgers Stop.

Hot water would be sourced from a rooftop solar hot water unit to be located next to solar power panels. The shower room would have a flat floor, falling away to outside the cottage. The water run-off would be collected in a water tank outside the cottage for garden irrigation. The shower room would be located next to the toilet. Kevin would install a septic tank to take care of his human waste. Electric power for lighting would be sourced from a power lead connected to Steven's machinery shed located nearby.

During times when the sky was overcast, he would rely on a small electric power generator located outside to heat the electric thermostat to provide hot water, light and power if Steven's electrical supply failed. Noise would not be a problem because it would be his noise, and the cottage would be located a fair distance away from Steven's place, although Kevin ultimately bought and installed a low-noise generator.

All in all, it was a simplistic design, having high comfort with minimal running cost. It would be painted in colours that would blend in with the surrounding bush. There was no need for council to approve construction plans because they would build it themselves, and only Kevin would live in it (except for the occasional visitor). No plumbing and drainage approval would be needed because they would not connect to the public system, and they would not require connection to the power grid.

The last part of the agreement was that when Kevin passed away, the ownership of the cottage would default to Steven and Annette. Kevin became very enthusiastic about Kevie's' Cottage. He wanted it constructed as soon as practically possible. His unbridled enthusiasm put a strain on his relationship with Steven and Annette, and between Steven and Annette.

Kevin would, more often than not, be using their telephone to contact people he was acquainted with in the building trades to come to his rescue with cheap materials and labour. There was always someone out there in supply or installation who owed Kevin a favour, or simply wanted to help him out because he was *a good man*.

And so construction started two months after Kevin and Steven shook hands on the deal. It took five more months before the cottage would be habitable. Both Steven and Annette were very happy to see it completed and for Kevin to move in. At least he was now out of their way.

Kevin found it difficult at first to settle into Kevie's Cottage. There were all these new sounds, night and day, that he had to get used to. When he awoke during the night or early morning, he had to orientate himself again. He thought he would get used to the new sounds and the challenging orientation issues, but he had a lot of trouble with the isolation. Kevin is a gregarious man. He must be with people. He must be able to converse. He wants to be everyone's best friend, including family members. He yearns for dialogue. All of this was missing in his new no-steps, camouflaged The Odgers Stop cottage.

#

When Kevin came to stay with us for the second time, he would always be hovering around us like a helicopter each afternoon when he came home from the club. Anne became frustrated because there was no "me time", so she laid down several simple rules for Kevin to follow so that Anne and I would not lose our connectivity. These rules where:

Rule 1: When you come home, please go straight to your room and have a rest.

Rule 2: Please do not come upstairs until after six p.m. each day.

Rule 3: Come up happy.

Anne never laid down any rules unless she explained why they were necessary in the first place. She explained to Kevin that we needed wife-and-husband time together after each day's work, to have that level of communication, so no person should come between us. There were certain issues that a wife and her husband needed to talk through and no one else should be privy to those conversations.

I could see that Kevin was a bit put out by my wife's assertiveness, but this was an issue he could not, and should not, negotiate. For the next few weeks, Kevin complied with Anne's request, but as time slipped past us all, he would come to the bottom of the stairs earlier and earlier each day, before six o'clock, and cry out, "Can I come up now?"

Anne would then look at me, roll her eyes, and, knowing that we would be shortly departing on an ocean cruise, relent and call out, "Come up Kevin; the coast is clear!"

#

Kevin decided one day, after living in his cottage for several weeks, that he would invite his best friend Les (Leslie) over for a few drinks, and maybe to stay the night. He needed company. He was feeling lonely. He forgot to tell Steven of his plans.

Les arrived on sundown, with a carton of cold ones, planning to stay the night. Les' son had driven him to Kevie's cottage and then left him to his own devices. Kevin and his best friend had a good night together. When the last beer bottle was emptied in the early hours of the morning, they both headed off to bed and passed out.

Steven sensed that his father had company overnight, but he didn't know who it was. Steven was upset that Kevin didn't let him know that a stranger would be staying on his property overnight. Steven waited until the visitor was picked up by a car late that same afternoon, then he headed to Kevie's cottage.

Steven entered the cottage to see Kevin placing the last empty beer bottle, upside down, into the empty cardboard carton on the floor.

"Who was that?" he demanded of Kevin.

"Les stayed overnight. I needed some company."

"Never liked him; he's a sponge."

Kevin looked at Steven in bewilderment.

Steve then commanded, "You need to tell me when someone stays. It's my property. I own this place with its liabilities."

Kevin became angry. "I haven't seen any pension money from you since I moved in," he countered in the growing argument between them.

"Stay on the subject," cried Steven.

"Well, while we're on the subject, Les'll be stayin' here with me for the next few months 'til he finds a place. His son is movin' interstate," Kevin informed him.

Steven stared at his father in anger, turned on his heel and stormed out of the cottage.

Neither man spoke to the other for the next few days. Kevin remained in his cottage.

Steven stayed in his home and went to and from work each day.

The following Saturday, Les moved in. Kevin called Steven on his mobile phone and left the following voice message. "Steven, we need to talk. I'll see ya out back Sunday mornin' for a cuppa."

Kevin awoke early that appointed Sunday morning. It had become a ritual that they would meet each Sunday morning to discuss football results and negotiate the coming week. He didn't know this would be his last Sunday spent in his cottage.

He got out of bed and put the kettle on the stove ready to make his favourite brew. He needed to converse. He checked to see if Les was still sleeping. Les had already departed for a day out with his son. Kevin then showered and changed into the attire for the day. He asked himself if he was feeling grumpy. Steven had called him *Mr Grumpy* several Sundays ago, and every Sunday since. That accusation stuck in his mind. He didn't feel grumpy that Sunday morning. Today he was feeling calm.

Kevin sat on his front porch sipping his first brew of the day, listening to the birds in the gum trees surrounding his cottage. There were flocks of starlings, sparrows, rainbow lorikeets, and of course, the usual murder of crows. They were all heralding in a brand-new day. He felt relaxed. He reminisced about going back on the road. He missed the adventure. He missed the excitement of meeting someone new each day.

Kevin looked at his watch. It was almost time to meet Steven. He made a second brew, put on his scuffs and headed up to Steven's place. As Kevin arrived on Steven's back verandah, he became worried because Steven wasn't there. *That's a bit odd*, he thought to himself, because Steven was always on time for anything. He was very punctual. Kevin didn't want to disturb them if they were still sleeping or catching up on things, so he sat down on his usual seat and again looked around at the gum trees, listening to the birds, trying to spot their variety.

It was a half hour later that he could hear movement inside the house. Then minutes later, Steven arrived at their regular meeting place.

"We had a big night, sorry, Kevie," said Steven as he negotiated through the back screen door with two mugs of black coffee in hand.

Kevin scolded Steven with some salty words. "Geez Steven, you're always on time. What's the bloody matter with ya?" The words surprised Kevin, as he hadn't intended for them to come out that way.

Steven looked at him with anger and didn't reply. They both sat there in silence for a while.

Several minutes later, after Steven had finished his coffee, the anger and frustration that he had been feeling for weeks came out in the form of an angry verbal barrage focused on Kevin. The verbal spray morphed into physicality as Steven's strong right arm came smashing across everything sitting on the table in front of Kevin. The nightmare for Kevin had begun.

Shocked with what he had just witnessed, Kevin jumped up from his chair and hastily retreated to his cottage, shaking from the confusion he was now feeling. He lay on his bed and wept. Later that morning, as he was still, lying in bed, he saw a note pushed under his door. It was a handwritten eviction notice signed by Steven and his wife. He did not recognise the handwriting. It was not Steven's writing.

Kevin rose to his feet and went to his window. He saw Steven walking away from the cottage, heading towards his own place. Kevin moved to his front door, opened it and yelled towards Steven, "What's this?" as he waved the eviction notice in one hand.

Steven stopped, turned and yelled back, "Get out! You've got 'til sundown to get out!"

#

Kevin awoke the morning after the eviction. He was some 30 kilometres north of Bishops Bridge, parked in a highway rest zone. Stunned, he surveyed his surroundings. *How did I get here?* he asked himself. His memory of the morning before started to return. He saw the eviction note lying on the passenger seat. He sobbed, and then sobbed some more.

After a long time grieving, thinking that he had nowhere to go, he decided to keep pushing north until he came to a fork in the road. This drive seemed to him to be a long one. Every road has a fork, but this road kept going and going ahead of him. He stopped. Confused, he decided to rest. He slept. He awoke from a nightmare scene of what he had suffered the day before. Steven was yelling at him with words he could not decipher.

Steven's strong right arm came smashing across everything sitting on the verandah table.

He did not notice that twilight had crept up and enveloped him. As he was lying on his mattress trying to clear his head and again wiping his eyes, a police car pulled up ahead of him.

"You in there! Wake up fella! You can't squat here," commanded a voice of authority.

Kevin sat up and opened his curtain to see a police officer staring at him through the windscreen of his van. He opened his side window and exclaimed, "I'm not squattin'!"

The policeman moved over to the side window and commanded, "Driver's licence please."

After some time, Kevin found his licence, alighted from his van, and handed it to the police officer.

This on the road episode ended up with the police officer, after discovering Kevin's disability when he asked him to alight from the van, allowing Kevin to rest up.

"He couldn't do enough for me, once he realised I had this little leg problem," chuckled Kevin, pointing to his skinny legs as he told Anne and me this story one afternoon on our verandah.

Kevin felt a little elated that he had not been fined for parking illegally. The next day, he decided to keep heading north to see what a fork in the road would bring. He needed to get far, far away from the nightmare of two days ago. He still could not process what had happened.

After several more hours of travelling, he finally came to a fork in the road. The sign on the east side of the fork stated *Brisbane*. The sign on the west side of the fork stated *Toowoomba*. He decided to turn east.

After driving for what seemed like many hours, Kevin steered his white van around a neighbourhood corner, then proceeded halfway up the street, and parked under a golden melaleuca tree, so escaping from the biting rays of brilliant sunshine. The blue sky of the morning had given way to a series of brilliant white fluffy clouds, roaming like Brown's cows, coming in from the south. The atmosphere was close due to the high humidity at that time of year. It had not rained for many weeks, which was unusual. Kevin looked at the grass on the footpath. It was a crunchy brown.

He sat there at the wheel for a little while collecting his thoughts and composure. He raised his mobile phone, put his glasses on, and then dialled a telephone number. He could hear the sound his call was making on another telephone close by. He let it ring for the usual eight cycles. There was no answer. He hung up.

He alighted from his white van with a haphazard movement, walking away from the house he had parked outside. He took several steps forward, then turned sideways, then turned again, so his final manoeuvre had him facing the house he intended to visit.

He stood still, holding onto the side of his white van, and then looked over at the house. He gazed at his phone. He grabbed his thick black walking stick from the front seat of his white van, and so proceeded to move towards the front gate with some difficulty because the terrain was uneven due to the tree roots of the golden melaleuca tree raising the ground around it.

He stopped under the tree after negotiating the kerb. He looked up to the upper front verandah of the house he was facing. He could see there was someone there but couldn't make out if it was one or two people. The verandah handrail slats provided good cover from prying eyes.

He continued his awkward approach, moving across the uneven tree-rooted footpath to finally reach the front gate. As he approached, one of the people sitting on the upper front verandah stood up. Kevin put his mobile phone into his hip pocket and yelled, with a booming voice that all the neighbourhood could hear, "Hi Chris and Anne! It's Uncle Kevie! I tried to ring youse to let youse know I was comin'! No answer!"

Kevin had arrived at our house. Friday night's dream on Saturday told was unfolding.

Chapter 11
Break Away

We returned home from enjoying seven days of separation from Kevin. I felt reinvented. I realised back then that I would be able to withstand my uncle's idiosyncratic nature. As I turned our car into its port, I noticed Kevin was sitting on our upper front verandah. This was unusual because it was mid-morning. Normally, at this time, he would be enjoying a coffee and a read of his newspaper at the local café.

Kevin noticed our arrival and came downstairs to greet us. "All went well?"

"We had a good time, Kevie," answered Anne as I was unpacking the vehicle.

Kevin helped me carry several items to our front door. "I'll let ya take that up," he said as he put the items down.

"Thanks," I said as I picked them up and then moved upstairs.

An hour later, after unpacking, we joined Kevin on our front verandah. It was too early for a cold one or a rum and Coke, so I asked, "Coffee anyone?"

Kevin replied with, "There's a bar open somewhere in the world right now—I'll have a cold one!"

So I obliged. I served Anne a cup of coffee.

I abstained until Kevin looked at me with his standard one-eyed Rooster Cogburn look and said, "No one should drink alone!" So I went and filled my left hand with a cold one.

As I sat down, Snoopy joined us. He lay under Kevin's seat and went immediately to sleep. I enquired, "Everything go all right, Kevie, while we were away?"

"Good as gold," he replied. I wasn't sure if he was replying to my enquiry or reacting to his first sip of his beer.

Anne then piped up. "Did you have any trouble while we were away for the week, Kevin?"

He looked over to her and replied, "We had rain while youse were away, and the animals are all fine—all good. I knew youse were comin' back this mornin', so I didn't do me usual coffee and paper trip."

We also experienced rain on our seven-day sojourn. It had rained for six out of the seven days, but the rain didn't dampen our spirits. We found plenty of places to go, things to do and people to meet.

As Anne and Kevin continued their conversation, I decided to go for a walk to inspect the condition of our flowers, vegetables and plants. Anne caught my eye as I moved back inside. I understood from her glance that she knew what I was going to do.

I returned ten minutes later. I gave Anne the thumbs up as I moved through the threshold. Kevin was looking east at the time. They must have run out of conversation, so I said, "All's in order—thanks, Kevie." Kevin turned his head and gave me a smile.

We were all in good spirits at this time. I raised the issue of an ocean cruise we were planning for later on in the year. We wondered if Kevin would look after our goods and chattels while we were away.

"I've got no place ta go," was his reaction, so we booked our passage the next day.

#

Several weeks later we arose very early on the morning of our ocean cruise departure. We were welcomed by brilliant sunshine and a slight easterly breeze coming in from the bay. We needed to rise early to ensure we had everything packed away for the ocean cruise, including the various medications people of our age require just to stay alive (it was the other way round when we were young—recreational drugs only).

Our cruise was scheduled to leave by sundown. We were allocated an early boarding time, and a final boarding time. The cruise duration was to be fifteen nights, so we would not use our car to take us to port. I agonised over which carriage service to best get us to port to ensure we would arrive on time.

We had always used a local taxicab owner, but he has retired now. He on-sold his cab after the taxi industry was seriously affected by ride-sharing businesses such as Uber. We had never used Uber or the like before, and at our age, it is always difficult for us to try new things. I said to Anne the night before departure, "Let's stay with what we know and book a cab. What could go wrong?" Anne agreed, so I booked the taxicab using their app.

I carried our bags and suitcases, one at a time, downstairs and left them waiting in the carport for the taxi driver, so she, or he, would not be stalking our street trying to identify our house number (most homes in our street have faded house numbers, including ours).

The cab arrived on time, which was a bit of a surprise. We are used to most taxis arriving much later than the scheduled time. The driver was a local. He parked on the opposite side of the road to where he needed to be. I went outside, stood in the carport next to our suitcases and signalled for him to drive over to where I was standing. He looked at me as if my hand signals and yelling were foreign to him.

So I crossed our suburban street and requested that he move his cab to the front of our house, because "my wife has a disability so she cannot cross the street". This he understood, and, with a twist of his Merv Hughes moustache, obliged me. He alighted from his vehicle and opened the passenger doors and luggage boot. He then stood there looking at me with his arms folded.

"Would you please load up the luggage?" I requested.

"Oh, sorry, sorry!" he said and commenced post-haste to do what I requested in a very haphazard way.

"Do you know where the cruise terminal is?" I asked.
"Oh, yes, yes," he responded with a broad smile.

"We need to get there by three p.m. today at the latest," I added.

"No worries," he said confidently.

As my exchange with the cab driver was going on, Anne came to the carport, assisted by Kevin, who was having as much trouble maintaining his balance as Anne was. I intervened.

Anne grabbed my arm and I steadied her. I then led her to the back seat of the cab.

Kevin was not far behind. Once Anne was settled, Kevin leaned into the cab and gave her a kiss on the cheek and told her not to worry. So Anne worried even more. Kevin returned upright, shook my hand and said, "Don't worry 'bout a thing. Snoop Dog and I will take care of everythin'."

I forgot to say goodbye to Snoop, I thought. I turned around and coaxed the big Welsh corgi to come.

I gave him a big cuddle, and then said, "See you later, big fella. Make sure you look after Kevie."

Anne called out from inside the taxi, "Bye Snoop!"

Snoopy was bewildered. He didn't know what to make of our departure.

As the cab took off with us inside, heading the wrong way, Kevin came out to wish us "bon voyage". Snoopy was standing beside him. Although we didn't know it then, that was the last time Anne, and I would see Snoopy standing.

As we headed off in the cab, each looking forward to a glorious holiday on a big ship sailing the South Pacific, I remember feeling elated again that I would not have to deal with Kevin. I also felt a little bit guilty that I should feel this way. *After all, Kevin is family,* I recall saying to myself.

I then said to the driver, "Keep going straight ahead, then turn left, go down the end of the street, then turn right." He turned left instead of right at the second turn.

"Do a U-turn. You should know where you're going from there."

He obliged, and we were then heading in the correct direction towards the river.

It seemed to me this driver must be new to the taxi business, so I asked, "Is this your first fare?"

He took a quick look at me and replied, "No, no. I've been drivin' for a coupla' weeks now."

That response surprised me because he still had not turned on the meter. I said, "Don't you think you need to start the meter?"

Without saying anything, he reached to the dashboard and turned on the meter.

We sat for a while in silence until I realised he was heading the wrong way again. "It's the mouth of the *river* port we need to go, not the city port."

He stopped the taxi. As we pulled up on the side of the road, he said, "What's the address? I'll need to put it into the navigation system."

"So you've never been to the river port before?" I asked.

"No," he said.

"That makes two of us," I replied.

"What's the address?" he again requested.

"I don't have the street address, but it is known as the Grain Terminal," I offered. "The ship's too big to come up the river."

With that information, he fiddled with his navigation system and off we went again.

My estimate of thirty to forty-five minutes for the drive was elapsing, so I asked, "How far now, driver?"

He glanced at me and said, "I don't know. We're back to where we started at the end of the freeway."

"You must have taken a wrong turn," I said, thinking the scenery looked familiar. "We need to head east towards the river."

So off we went again. Ten minutes later we were back at the same location at the start of the freeway.

"There are some construction workers over there. Go ask them which way to go," I demanded.

The driver got out of his taxi, walked over to the construction workers, and I could then hear a little bit of discussion, with a lot of fingers pointing east.

The driver returned. "Got it sorted," he said confidently. So off we went yet again.

Ten minutes later we were back at the same spot for the third time.

"There's a shop over there. Go ask them which way to go," I commanded in frustration.

The driver got out of his taxi, walked over to the shop and disappeared into its entry.

After what seemed like another ten minutes, he appeared again, with a can of cola in hand. He returned to the cab. "Should be OK now. We need to turn right up ahead where the sign says 'Port'," he said confidently.

Fifteen minutes later, for the fourth time, we were back at the same spot yet again, after passing by the construction workers and the cola shop.

"This is ridiculous!" cried Anne from the back seat. "Call into your controller and ask them which way to go, driver!"

And so he did. Now, if I were the driver, I would have ensured the conversation with my controller could not be heard by my passengers, but I wasn't the driver. He left his loudspeaker on, and we heard the controller say, "You go under the overpass, you dick, not over the overpass!"

Seems the cab had been going around in circles, on and off the freeway. The construction workers all waved to us as we passed them by, several times. I noticed they had lifted their construction hats and were laughing as we passed them by for the last time.

Finally, we headed in the correct direction, moving under the overpass. There was a great sigh of relief from the back seat. After travelling for five minutes, we came into clear view of a big cruise ship waiting for us at the Grain Terminal.

#

We arrived at the Grain Terminal ten minutes before our final embarkation time. The driver pulled up in front of the entry, stopped the meter and said, "That'll be $250 please."

I was fuming. "The fare should be around $70. You took us for a ride! I'm not paying for what amounts to four trips to one destination," I yelled.

He could see that I was upset, but then he upset me further by saying, "If you don't pay, I'll have to pay. I'm just the driver. I don't own the taxicab."

Anne bellowed from the back seat, "And you don't know where you are going! It's unreasonable that you expect us to pay for your inexperience. There's a consumer law against that!"

The driver dropped his head.

"I will pay $100 dollars, no more," I offered. The driver accepted, and then drove off in a huff.

The consolation for us arriving late was that all other passengers were checked in. We were the last of the 2200 passengers to move through the embarkation line. By the time we were checked in (the quickest time we have ever experienced), we were exhausted, possibly because of the turmoil of the cab ride and the anxiety that came with it.

"I need a stiff drink," pleaded Anne as we moved through the metal detectors, the last part of check in procedure, so we headed to the first bar we came across (I like to have a drink at each bar on a cruise ship, so this was a good start).

#

As we entered the bar area, a voice called out, "Hello Anne!"

It was the Pitts (the Pitt family, not *the pits*). We had not seen them since junior football days when both our families were part of the same team. It was a pleasant surprise for all of us, and we sat with them and had several stiff drinks together, sharing stories, including our taxi debacle, and reminiscing about bygone days.

We then told the Pitts we needed to unpack and get ready for the ship's safety instructions demonstration, so we departed and headed towards the lifts. As we were making our way, a voice called out, "Hello Anne!" It was our family doctor's receptionist. When Anne was a day-care mother, she had looked after the receptionist's two children for several years. Talk about it being "a small world after all"!

Anne was well known in our neighbourhood as "Mother Duck and her ducklings", because they would all walk, hand-in-hand, single file, no matter where they went, with Anne up front guiding them all. We exchanged pleasantries with the receptionist for several minutes, and then excused ourselves as we had to unpack and not miss the safety demonstration.

The ship was so large that we never saw the Pitts again on that voyage. We did bump into the receptionist several times, so it would seem we had similar interests. We enjoyed the ambience and spaciousness of the ship. It was well presented and comfortable.

#

We enjoyed occupying our cabin, which had an external balcony, although one major problem was with Anne's assisted walker. It would not move freely through the cabin threshold because the rear wheel axle was too wide. I needed to collapse the walker each time we went in or out of our cabin. This created balance issues for Anne because she had nothing to hold onto. With this came high anxiety each time.

If I have a complaint to make about the ship, it would not be about the ship itself, it would be about the manners left at home by most able-bodied passengers. They would not use the access stairs located beside the lifts. They would take front position in the lobby, thus causing disabled people to wait until the lobby was cleared of able-bodied people. I was disgusted to see this happening each day, so this led to many heated discussions between me and able-bodied passengers. I guess I endeared myself to each of them, because they would acknowledge me when they walked past, but never engaged me in conversation.

This problem was also prevalent in the theatre. Able-bodied people would take up disabled people's seats because they were so obese, they couldn't walk down several steps to access the usual seating. I guess they saw themselves as disabled because of their size. During these times of rising resentment, I recalled one of Kevie's' quotes which went something like, "Life is full of karma so treat others as you would have them treat you otherwise it would come back to you and bite you hard on ya bum". Recalling Kevie's' quote assisted me to manage my fleeting anger during these times of frustration on the cruise.

#

After attending the safety demonstration, we decided to go forward as the ship made its way through the mouth of the river and into the bay. As we walked forward, the grey clouds overhead reflected in the water below us, then gave way to a brilliant reflection of sunshine. We arrived at the bow of the ship in time to see several dolphins racing beside us towards open sea. The dolphins frolicked in and out of the water and occasionally cut across our bow.

We decided to go back to our cabin to see if we could observe the dolphins from our balcony. As we entered, I collapsed Anne's walker and assisted her to our external balcony. The dolphins were nowhere to be seen. We sat out on the balcony for a while, enjoying the view and plotting our next move. "Let's see the map to see where we're going," said Anne. I stood up and obliged.

Our first port of call was listed as Alotau in Papua New Guinea, followed by Milne Bay, Kirwina Island and then Rabaul. That would conclude our visit to Papua New Guinea. The ship would then turn around and head for the South Pacific, where we were scheduled to stop at Luganville, followed by Vila, then Noumea. All in all, the cruise would stretch over fifteen nights.

We were excited at the prospect of seeing the islands and ports of Papua New Guinea, where we had never been before, and returning to eastern Melanesia, which we had visited many times before and both loved. We were hoping the ports we were destined to visit in Papua New Guinea would be accessible for Anne, as they proved to be in the South Pacific.

Anne didn't feel well later that afternoon (I suspected because of the taxi driver), so she stayed in our cabin while I went to formal dinner alone to meet our fellow travellers. It was a pleasant night spent over a three-course meal and some very good table wines.

When I first arrived at the dinner table, I noticed that our fellow travellers were talking in their own small groups. I guessed it was because they had not been formally introduced to each other. *What would Uncle Kevie do?* I thought to myself as I surveyed this social isolation. So I *did a Kevie* and took control of the table by introducing myself to each one of them. I let them know my wife was not well, and then asked each person their name and where they were from. I was elated. I felt that some of my uncle's people skills had surfaced within me. Kevie's' technique of getting people to open up had rubbed off on me. Kevin would often say, "Most people are shy or reserved, or both, so it is up to you to break the ice by asking the first question. Marvel how the ice melts!" So using one of Kevie's' many people-management techniques, I brought all fellow travellers into a common conversation.

Towards the end of the dinner, I could see that most of the personal barriers that had been present when I first arrived at the dining table had dissolved. There was much vibrant laughter when amusing stories were told. The night was getting late, and dinner had concluded, so I gave my apologies to my new-found friends and left the table, promising that more lively conversation would continue the following night.

#

I returned to our stateroom to find the lights out, but that Anne could not sleep. So I changed into my sleep wear and lay in bed talking with her. This seemed to calm her down, but we neither of us had a good night's rest.

The following morning, I awoke to Anne asking, "What time is it?"

I mumbled something I can't recall, felt around for my phone, looked at its face and said, "Nine o'clock. Time to get up?"

"Yes. I can't sleep any more, my mind is all over the place. I need to go for a walk," she replied.

So we got out of bed, showered separately and dressed for the day. We left our cabin and headed for the catered breakfast, which was located four decks above us on the top level of the ship.

As we moved towards the lift lobby, I said to Anne, "Not too many people around."

Anne stopped at the lift, pressed the call button, and said, "They're probably all still sleeping. It's only us idiots that are up looking for breakfast."

"Probably," said I as we entered the lift.

We arrived at the catered breakfast level and walked into the dining room. *Where are all the people?* I thought again as we found a comfortable table for two. The waiter came over and asked if we required coffee. "Yes, please, black for two," I replied, then asked,

"What time is it?"

"Six a.m., sir, we have just now opened," he replied.

I looked around and found the ship's clock on the far wall. The correct time was confirmed. My phone had apparently moved to Greenwich Mean Time for some reason overnight, and I had read nine p.m. as nine a.m. Anne and I do not usually arise until around nine each day, so getting up at six was a big shock for our systems.

Anne and I laughed at our time-travel misadventure. It made me feel good to see her smiling again. After a hearty breakfast, with the two of us dining alone, we went back to our cabin and slept for several more hours. It was noon by the time we realised it.

"Hungry? Want something to eat?" I asked as I wiped sleep from my eyes.

"No," she said, and then asked, "Do you think the casino might be open?"

I sensed dejection in her first response, so I answered her question with, "Well, let's go and have a look-see!" And so we did.

We walked into a large ritzy, glitzy room named *The Casino*. There were wall-to-wall poker machines beckoning "come play with me" using flashing lights, enticing voice phrases, and popular themes from movies, songs and games. I could tell Anne was hooked from the time she first walked under the casino sign above the entry.

Anne is the responsible gambler in our relationship. I don't mind playing an odd Keno game here or there, but I cannot sit there feeding a hungry machine with my cash. I don't mind Anne playing the machines because, believe it or not, they are therapeutic for people suffering from various

Parkinson's conditions caused by a lack of dopamine in the brain.

Dopamine is a natural chemical produced in our brains. Production is vital to each of us to maintain the mental and physical relationship in our bodies, vitally more so for people suffering from the Parkinson's disorders. A lack of dopamine brings on zombie-like conditions, although I must say that I have observed people playing poker machines who look like they are in a zombie mode even if they do not have Parkinson's.

The casino manager passed by us as we were trying to understand if the casino was open. I called to him as he moved past and asked, "Excuse me, what time does the casino open?"

"In about two hours, sir," was his polite response.

Anne looked dejected again. She was very eager to play. You can see a change in her demeanour when she has had some time on a machine. I suggested we start our bar crawl and come back in two hours' time.

My suggestion was taken up eagerly, so we moved in and out of three bars. I ticked these off my bar-crawl list as we arrived back at the casino. We were both in a far better frame of mind because the alcoholic drinks were doing their intended job. We came across a poker machine that Anne liked (she has a way of looking at a machine and then knowing whether it is a good one or not). I helped her onto her seat, parked her assisted walker, asked if she was comfortable, then went over to the bar to see if I could find some finger food for both us. The bar served various nuts in a bowl, as well as warm party pies, sausage rolls, and the like, but only if you were a player. As I was explaining to the bartender that my wife was over there playing that machine and had requested something to eat, an intoxicated middle-aged man came out of nowhere and stumbled over to the bar, sitting uncomfortably close beside me.

He looked at me and dribbled, "How ya' goin'!"

"Going well," I politely replied, hoping he would not engage me in conversation—but he did.

As I ordered a rum and Coke from the bartender, my bleary-eyed new friend asked, "You gotta drinks package?"

"Sorry—what was that?" I asked, bewildered.

"You know—gotta' drinks package? You goin' deaf or somethin'!" he snarled as he lost his balance and so slid towards my left ear. *What would Kevie do in this predicament?* I thought.

I then said, "Yes, I am going deaf—so my uncle tells me. What's a drinks package?" I said in a friendly way, not knowing whether this drunk was getting lethal or not.

"You don't have any drinks package?" was my new friend's response. "You need to go and git yerself one. You can buy one anytime. Gives you $60 worth of drinks a day. I've bin tryin' to catch up on my quota all day—I'm still only halfway there!" he said with some boast in his delivery, as the bartender handed me my rum and Coke.

"I think you're sozzled," I said under my breath as I signed my drinks purchase.

"You're cacky-handed!" my inebriated friend exclaimed, as if he had discovered gold.

"All my life—and loving it," I defended.

He commenced lecturing me on how inferior I was being left-handed, in the same fashion as my uncle, who would often tease me about it.

As my new-found drunken friend went through his superior machinations, a series of montages shot through my brain. It was as if the last minute of my life had arrived, and I was in judgement of myself. I remember before I started to go to school, when my family and I went to visit my great-grandmother, she would often say to me, "Being left-handed is the devil's work. Use your right hand at school!"

At home, my father would often tease me with names such as cacky-hander, and southpaw. I didn't realise these were derogatory terms until I attended school.

School was a big challenge for me. Apart from standing out because I am left-handed, I was self-conscious, and so very shy. If I was walking on my way to school and someone was coming my way, I would cross to the other side of the street to avoid them, so there needn't be any eye contact or shared dialogue.

I remember when I was at the public primary school, a teacher used a ruler many times to slap the knuckles of my left hand to try to force me to use the other hand. Later on, in a private primary school, the meanest teacher used a thick leather strap over the back of my head because I was a sinner in the eyes of the Christian Brothers. Many have tried to save me through my life, but I have refused to conform.

All those teachers who were brutal to me would tell me they were being kind to me because, if I persisted with using my left hand, I would have learning difficulties throughout my whole life. Despite the continual methods used by teachers to force change in me, I found it very difficult to live in a right-handed world.

After graduating from school, I discovered that left-handed people make up around only ten per cent of the world's population, so the other ninety per cent of the population dictate the design of access into buildings, motor vehicles, tools, instruments, gadgets and the like to make life easier for them, but not for me. This, of course, causes much grief for lefties.

There have been many famous people in our history who were, or are, left-handed. I was pleasantly surprised to learn this one day in the ship's library. Leonardo Da Vinci was a famous engineer and artist. Famed movie stars include Jim Carrey, Tom Cruise, Robert De Niro, Morgan Freeman, Whoopi Goldberg, Angelina Jolie, Nicole Kidman, Brad Pitt, Julia Roberts, and Chewbacca the Wookie.

There are famous left-handed writers such as Lewis Carroll, Bill Bryson, Germaine Greer, Berthold Schwartz, Janet Street Porter and Uhland Ludwig. Famed royalty, include the Queen Mother and Prince William.

Famed singers and musicians include Celine Dion, Paul McCartney, Ricky Martin and Sting.

Politicians include Barack Obama, George Bush and Winston Churchill. I was thinking that I felt very privileged to be in such esteemed company, and then I was drawn back to ship's reality.

My new-found drunken friend must have decided he had made enough fun of me, so said, out of the blue, "Nice meetin' ya, leftie," and then staggered away to find some unawares passenger to spoil their day. It must have been because I looked so very blank as my mind was going through the left-handed montage of my life, that he departed, looking for an unsuspecting traveller to torment.

I walked over to Anne with some nibbles, and two drinks. She was bright-eyed and having a ball. She was winning. She was shining. I gave her most of the nibbles (I had eaten while entertaining my friend at the bar). I suggested we might take out her winnings and have a nap, and then come back to gamble later, after dinner and the show. She agreed, which surprised me (*Still a little anxious from the taxi ride*, I thought). Most of that afternoon was spent in the cabin having a nap, watching television, showering and changing for dinner.

#

We watched the sun set over the navy blue, choppy water from our balcony, then decided it was time to go to dinner. As we arrived at the dinner table, I introduced Anne to our new friends, and then asked them as we sat down, "Are we on time?"

Dinner was up to its usual high standard of good quality food, table wines and stories told around the table. Our earlier misfortune was a highlight of the conversation. Before too long, it was time to go to the theatre to enjoy a new ship's company production.

The show was a most entertaining, two-hour production of music, dancing and singing. Of all the female dancers on stage, one stood out for me. She was an exceptional dancer and beautiful singer. I thought she should have had top billing. She sang like an angel.

The next two days were sea days (no ports of call), so we entertained ourselves by going on a morning walk on the top open deck of the ship, attending a catered breakfast (at a reasonable time), having hot dogs or hamburgers beside the pool during lunch hour, and then off to our formal dinner. We did not attend the theatre on the second night at sea because it was the same show as the night before, although I would have loved to see the angel again. Anne and I spent each evening in the casino where Anne found her enjoyment in front of a poker machine.

On our fourth day, we arrived in Port Alotau, so the casino would not be open on this day, nor would the theatre. We decided to go ashore after all the other passengers had disembarked. It was a taxing time for Anne to do this, but she did it. She will never tell you she is exhausted because of her Parkinson's. She has true grit. "A tough old bird," Kevin would often remark.

After disembarking, we moved along the jetty heading to the markets, which were located on the other side. As we approached, I noticed the angel had moved out of the markets and was walking toward us. As she approached, I thought *what would Kevie do?* I cleared my throat, brushed back my hair (what is still left on my head), sucked in my soft belly, and said a weak, "Hello."

She looked at me, a little bit shocked I think, and gave me a blank response. Blank responses are the story of my life. I remembered that not too many females found me attractive, even when I was young. The only reason Anne let me take her out the first time was to make her boyfriend jealous. He had broken off their relationship a week before. I think she first thought I was goofy, or cute, or something, because I played footsies with her under a dinner table shared by her friends, whom I didn't know.

We moved around the markets for a little while, but then decided it was not very accessible for either of us, so we headed back to the ship.

The next day, we arrived at Kirwina Island. This was exciting for us as we had never been there before. It is a pristine part of Papua New Guinea, and the first time any cruise ship had visited this paradise. We were looking forward to lying on the pure white sand under the glistening green palm trees and sampling a local brew.

We decided to go to the catered breakfast that morning so we could see if the port was accessible for people with a disability. It was not. The only way off the ship was along a rickety timber jetty, upon which there was a long single file of passengers going to shore. I thought the jetty would collapse under so much weight, given the large number of obese sightseers moving slowly in single file.

When breakfast was consumed, we went to the disco level, located on top of the ship. It's where the midnight discos are held each night while cruising. This level of the ship provides panoramic views, and it has a bar. There would be no one in the disco at that time. They would all be ashore. We would have the place to ourselves, and we did, but the bar was not open.

Anne made herself comfortable on a sofa in front of the large window facing the bow. I went down one deck, to the pool level bar, ordered our favourite drinks, and returned as quickly as I could to take in the delightful views.

We could easily see the tourists moving off the rickety jetty, some with ease, and others with mobility difficulty, onto the pure white beach, which gave the appearance of compressed snow. From there, the tourists were organising a canoe ride, the only activity on the beach. There were two-person canoes all the way up to ten-person canoes.

I said to Anne, as we were observing the tourists, "No way would we have rented a canoe. They don't have outriggers."

Anne asked, "What do you mean by that?"

I explained that an outrigger was a small parallel floating device attached to the canoe that keeps a canoe stable. "You could easily stand up without the canoe capsizing," I said.

As we watched, small canoes started to come out from the beach, followed by bigger and bigger ones. The smaller canoes paddled to the ship, and then moved around it; others went exploring the cliff face that formed the southern entry to the beach.

We looked to our right, and suddenly we saw a large lady stand up inside a larger canoe. Facing towards us, she commenced to take photos. We could hear much yelling going on. Suddenly the canoe capsized. Other canoes came from everywhere! The locals came from everywhere! A lot of bodies were floating in the water.

The locals must have all had bronze medallion training, because they quickly got the floating tourists to the beach with no harm done. This safety episode (or lack thereof) was a big talking point around the ship later that day and night. Some people were laughing out loud, others where frowning (I guessed the frowners were the floating tourists).

The next two days were sea days, so our sea day routine kicked in again. Our sea day consisted of coffee in bed, followed by a formal breakfast (there would be far too many people at the catered breakfast so the formal breakfast was safer option for Anne); a walk around the ship (if we stumbled across a bar we had not previously been to, we stayed for drink and ticked it off our bar-crawl list); a stint in the casino; attendance at the formal lunch (again a much safer proposition for Anne); an afternoon power nap; watching a programme on television (usually the news), followed by attendance at the formal dinner, and then the theatre.

On port days, our routine would change to disembarkation and then lunch in some tavern close by. There would not be a show in the theatre that night, so we would spend some time in the casino before heading off to bed.

After one of the port days, Anne and I went to the casino that night. I made sure Anne was comfortable in front of a poker machine of her choice, and then I headed to the bar for drinks. Sitting at the bar was the angel. She took my breath away.

I delivered an enthusiastic Kevie-like, "Hello again!"

The angel looked at me with the same face I saw several days before and then turned away. This time there was a slight difference in her appearance. I noticed she had been crying.

"Are you all right?" I asked, genuinely concerned. "Yeah—just in and out of love stuff," she replied.

"I reckon you're the best performer on stage," I added.

"Thanks," she said unconvincingly, and then our conversation fell away.

The bartender came over and I ordered my usual rum and Coke, and a chardonnay for Anne.

"One more, *chérie*?" he enquired of the angel.

"Include that on my bill," I requested of the bartender. "Thank you!" said the angel, sounding much more convincing.

I looked at her and said, "You have a voice that is so heavenly. You sound like an angel on stage."

She stared back at me, thought for a little while, and then asked, "Have you ever had an out-of-body experience?"

I thought that was odd. Maybe she was entering into a depressive mood, or a little drunk, or both, so I decided to stay with her in conversation and delay the delivery of Anne's chardonnay.

I told the angel, "I played a game of football once. I wasn't very good at it, but on this day, I played out of my skin. It was as if I was floating above myself, looking down on my body as I moved forward and kicked a couple of goals—it was as if I was coaching myself from above."

The angel smiled at me and said, "You know, sometimes when you're singing, and you reach those impossible notes, the audience and the music fall away. Your spirit rises above. You cannot hear any other sound except the feedback from your voice reaching perfection." She stopped for a moment, and then continued, "When you reach that pinnacle of perfection, you can touch the face of God."

I could see that the angel, at one time during a performance, truly believed she had met God.

I was pleased with myself for having been able to get angel to open up to me, a stranger to her. *Must be Kevie's training kicking in again*, I thought.

Chapter 12
Sad Goodbye

Our cruise through Papa New Guinea was a pleasant one, but several of the ports were inaccessible for assisted walking, so we had no choice but to stay on board ship. We had expected Rabaul to be very accessible. The Americans constructed a concrete wharf there during the Second World War. It seems they had forgotten to construct a proper road from the wharf into town. The track to town was a mixture of rubble and compressed earth, which was very difficult for Anne to negotiate.

After my intimate conversation with the angel the night before, I never saw her again, nor did I find out her real name. She didn't appear on stage for any other performance. I never saw her around the ship for the duration of our voyage. I often, to this present day, wonder if she is all right.

The next morning, we awoke with both of us sharing a feeling of homesickness. Was Snoopy all right? Had Kevin been feeding him? Had Kevin burned the house down? We were due into Luganville port that afternoon, so I calmed Anne down by saying I would send a text message to our younger son Laurie from that port to ask him to call in home and check on things.

Several hours past, then I received a text message from Laurie stating that he had been to our house, that Snoopy was healthy, but looked lonely, and that Kevin wasn't there. The house was still standing. It had not burned down. We both breathed a little easier after receiving the news. Kevin was probably at the club when Laurie went to inspect. Laurie told us much later that he was contemplating taking Snoopy home with him until we returned home, but local council rules prohibit three dogs in one back yard, and Laurie has two dogs of his own.

So we were now in the South Pacific. The ports we were about to visit were familiar ports. We had been there several times before. The last time we visited Noumea, we walked the streets looking for a pub, or better still, a tavern. On our journey around town this time, we saw a sign on a building stating 'Casino'. We looked at each other and exclaimed, "That'll do!"

We walked into the casino only to discover it was a food supermarket, not a gambling place. So we walked the streets and ended up on the wrong side of town. We quickly turned around, headed back to the ship and spent that afternoon in the last bar to be ticked off on our bar-crawl list. It was then a very pleasant afternoon. We felt safe.

The next few days were the last days of the cruise. We were heading back home, so we were in sea-day mode. Nothing of interest happened on the ship during those last few days. We went to the formal breakfast, lunch and dinner, as we had done before. We went to the theatre (no angel). We had reached the point in our journey when we just wanted to be at home.

On the last night of our cruise, I received a text message from our elder son, Ben. He said that Kevin had been attempting to contact us. Snoopy was seriously ill. Ben said that he told Kevin to call the vet, but he didn't know whether Kevin had done that or not.

I returned a text message to Ben saying that we would be home by mid-morning the next day and I would take Snoopy to the vet once we arrived home if Kevin had not already done so.

Surely Snoopy is not that ill? He is only eleven years old. Cardigans go for thirteen to fifteen years, I puzzled.

I wasn't worried about Snoopy's health at that time because Snoopy was in good condition when we left to go cruising. We had only been away for fifteen days, and Laurie had been to check on him only a few days ago. *What could go wrong in just a few days?* I again puzzled. Anne became very worried.

We packed our bags and placed each in the corridor outside our cabin for collection and delivery to the wharf early the next morning. I circled an early departure time on our disembarkation card so that we could get to the airport in time to have breakfast before boarding our flight home. Neither of us slept well during that last night on board.

#

The ship's foghorn sounded several times, stirring us out of our slumber. We raised our heads from our pillows and looked at each other in a bewildered state. It took a little while for both of us to realise we had arrived back home. With a new-found energy, we showered, dressed, packed what little things we hadn't packed the night before, then made our way to the waiting lounge for disembarkation. By this time, we had entered the harbour and moved under the bridge. It was not long before we had moored. The fog, which had caused the horn to sound, had lifted.

Disembarkation was well rehearsed and rapid. We arrived inside the shipping terminal building in no time at all, collected our luggage and were then in a taxi heading off to the airport. Again, this cab ride was very unusual, not because we were lost en route again, but because the driver knew exactly where he was heading, and he had only one arm.

At the shipping terminal building, I wasn't sure if this driver would assist with the loading of our luggage into the taxi, but without asking, he was all over it. With his single arm, he swung the big cases, one at a time, up around his shoulders (he had two of those), then let each fall into place inside the luggage compartment of his taxicab. *He must have worked in Cirque du Soleil*, I thought to myself.

The cab ride was a short one to the airport, given that this driver knew exactly how to get there soonest. After checking in ready for our flight home, we enjoyed a hearty English breakfast. As I washed down that last of the bacon and eggs with a long black, Anne said, "Gee, I hope Snoopy's okay."

When you have been with someone over a long period of time, you tend to be able read your partner's mind and become a thought-sharer. You get to know instantly what the other is thinking. Quite often you blurt out the same thoughts converted to word. "I was thinking the very same thing," I replied. "We haven't heard any news from anyone. There are no text messages or voice messages on my phone, so Snoop must be all right."

Our flight home was on time to board, to depart, and to arrive at our home airport terminal. We collected our luggage and headed for the taxi rank, where several cabs were waiting for a fare. All taxi drivers possessed two arms at this terminal, and I was sure they knew where to go.

As we got onto the freeway (the same freeway where the first driver was lost, not once, but four times, on our way to our ocean cruise), my mobile phone rang. It was our younger son Laurie calling.

He said, "Kevin's just phoned to tell me Snoopy's pretty bad. Where are you?"

I was shocked. Anne looked shocked. Even though she could not possibly know what message I was receiving, I guess she could tell what was going down.

"We'll be there in about thirty minutes," was all that I could muster.

"Okay. I'll ring Kevin and let him know," said Laurie, and then hung up.

We sat silently for the rest of the journey. During what now seemed like a long cab ride, my thoughts were all about Snoopy, from the time we took him home at eight weeks old, to the time we last saw him before we left on this latest cruise adventure.

#

At eight weeks old, Snoopy was a ball of black-and-white fluff. He fitted neatly onto my hand. He was so small he could move under the bottom rail of our lower balcony balustrade. Before we took Snoopy home, we had to condition Elle to the idea that another dog would be living in her house. For several weeks before Snoopy arrived, I would say to Elle, "Snoopy's coming! Snoopy's coming!" I would then show her a picture of a black-and-white cardigan corgi.

Snoopy didn't sleep at all the first night he spent with us as a puppy, not because he was frightened, but because he wanted to explore. He sniffed here, and he sniffed there, and he weed here, and he weed there. I could hear the pads of his little paws contacting our colonial timber floors as he moved about our home.

For the first few weeks, Snoopy made several attempts to lie beside Elle, but she would not have anything to do with him. Then one day, Snoopy walked over to Elle, who was sitting Staffie style on our kitchen floor, and he lay down between her legs. She comforted him as if he were her own. From that day on, they endured a long mother-and-son relationship.

When Snoopy was old enough to chew, we gave him his first solid food in the form of a meaty bone. He eagerly took it outside and started to practise how to chew this new solid food. He spent a good hour devouring small pieces of flesh stuck to the bone, until he decided he was thirsty, so needed to find his bucket of water.

As Snoopy went around our back yard looking for his water bucket, a big black crow moved in and took his bone away. Snoopy was furious. He bolted towards the crow, snarling and barking his head off. The black crow decided it was a little bit risky staying at ground level, so grappled with the bone in its beak and then flew off. Snoopy was inconsolable. Not even a fresh new bone would cheer him up. From that day on, Snoopy never liked Mr Crow and would chase him at every opportunity.

As Snoopy grew, he would often challenge Elle to a foot race as we walked around the local playground and parkland surrounds. Their foot race would end up at the local creek, where Elle would be first to the water, time and time again. She would then go for a swim, but Snoopy would only look on. He didn't like water, except for drinking.

When Snoopy turned two years old, he finally won their foot race. He was so proud of himself! He strutted around the park with his chest stuck out and a big grin on his face.

#

My thoughts of Snoopy faded when Anne announced, "We're almost home," as we turned off the freeway and into our suburb. My mind was thumping, my heart was pounding. I found it very difficult to form any words in response to Anne's subliminal reassurance.

The taxi arrived at our front gate. Kevin's white van was nowhere to be seen. There was no vet vehicle parked outside. This scene added to my anxiety. I paid the driver and wished him well as I tried to stay composed, but Anne saw right through me and said, "Leave the luggage here. We'll get it later. Let's go find Snoopy."

We entered our house through the front door then moved through to the back yard. There, on the ground, lay Snoopy on his right side. Our worst fears were realised. His breathing was very shallow. His nose was so dry it looked like leather, and his fur was dry and brittle. He wanted to greet us home, but I could see he didn't have the energy to raise his head. He could only look straight ahead. He seemed to be in a lot of pain.

"I'll take him off to the vet," I said to Anne. I moved around Snoopy to determine how best to lift him up and carry him.

Suddenly the back door swung open with a crash and out came Kevin.

"The vet's on her way. I've just been up there to tell her how sick the big fella is. I don't think she believed me over the phone. She'll be here at three," he yelled, as if we were both standing at the far end of our back yard.

I cannot remember what I said to Kevin in return. I think I thanked him for being so concerned, but I just don't remember. My head was all over the place. I do remember Anne saying, "You stay with Snoop. I'll go and put a few things away."

So I sat down beside him, softly stroked his dry and brittle fur, and said reassuring words to him (words to also reassure me). I think I said something like, "You'll be all right now big fella. You're tough. The vet will be here soon to make it all better." Snoopy could only move his eyes, and his eyes were telling me that he was slowly slipping away.

Snoopy could always communicate with his eyes. He didn't need to bark much to grab my attention. When he wanted to go a particular way, his eyes would point in that direction, then back at me. When he wanted his breakfast or dinner, his eyes would be on the pantry. When walking him, if he became bored because I was talking to a neighbour for too long, he would look at me then his eyes would look towards the park or home.

The vet arrived right on three o'clock. I met her at our front door. She had no formalities to extend. The first thing she said to me was, "Tell me what you think is wrong with your man!" She always referred to Snoopy as a man, even when he was a puppy.

I told her we had just arrived home from our ocean cruise, but that Kevin could provide all the information she was seeking.

Kevin explained to her that Snoopy had been very ill, but only for one day, several weeks ago, and that he was up and walking the next day and eating his food the day after. He had only become ill again several days ago.

As Kevin continued to narrate, the vet was asking him various questions and poking and prodding Snoopy. She inserted a thermometer in his ear and in his rectum. I could see that she was very concerned for our *man*. "I'll give him a painkiller—he seems to be in great pain," she said as she administered the medicine. She then spent the next half hour examining Snoopy, and then called for a conference with us. She told us that she was not sure what the problem was, but that she had taken blood and saliva samples and would go back to the laboratory and see what she could discover. She asked me to call in later that day and she would give me more medicine "to get your man through the night".

As she said this, I looked over to Snoopy, who had raised his head and was looking at me with his sad eyes, which were telling me, "I'm scared—please help me!"

#

I saw that very same look only one other time in my life. It was a time when I was a young and foolish teenager. I only thought about myself back then. I was bulletproof. I had joined with some other young men to go kangaroo shooting. I made the mistake of placing my rifle in the back tray of the utility van—not securing it. We drove over some very rough terrain that day, so my rifle bounced all over the tray. By the time we stopped, I was intending to secure the rifle when someone yelled, "Roos on the hill!"

I looked to the west and there stood six big eastern greys. They were stationary, in silhouette as the sun was setting behind them. The rays of the sun must have acted like a spotlight shining on us, so these macropods were inquisitive. I reached for my rifle, aimed for the biggest of the mob, which I estimated must have been around two metres tall, and fired.

I could see through my rifle sights that my first bullet dug into the ground two metres to the right. None of the macropods moved. I realised my rifle sight settings were damaged from movement in the utility tray, so I compensated, and then fired a second shot. The bullet dug into the ground one metre from where the big macropod was standing. Again, there was no movement from the mob. Someone said, "You're gettin' close!" as I fired my third shot. The big macropod fell. The rest of the mob took off over the hill. The young men congratulated me for the kill.

My first kill, I thought, as blood rushed through my brain. My endorphins were running rampant. I was elated. I ran to the hill to witness my first pleasure kill. What I beheld changed my life. The big roo saw me coming, so tried to stand, but couldn't. My bullet had ripped through his chest and exited out his back, leaving a very large hole. There was blood and tissue everywhere. My hollow point bullet must have ruptured his heart. When he realised he could not move and that he was slipping away, he lay there and just looked at me with that very same look that Snoopy gave me. It was a look of sad, unexpected loss.

I stayed with the macropod as he passed away that sunset. I could not bring myself to shoot him again, even though my friends were yelling at me to end his suffering. I sat there with him, and we just looked at each other, until he took his last breath. I promised him as he passed that I would never ever go hunting for pleasure again. I never did from that day on.

#

I walked over to Snoopy and sat with him for a little while. I realised I needed to collect his medicine, so I said, "You'll be all right, big fella. No more pain now the vet has given you a painkiller. I'll go now and bring home some medicine to make you better."

Kevin said he would sit with Snoopy, so I helped Anne upstairs, made sure she was comfortable, and then headed to the vet surgery to collect Snoopy's medication. As I entered the surgery reception, I noticed their business name ended with the word "practice," which worried me.

"Any change?" I enquired of Kevin when I arrived home.

"He's about the same, but he doesn't seem to be in pain," replied Kevin. "I'll stay with him. You go an' look after Anne," he added. So I did.

Night descended quickly. Anne and I needed to sleep after a very stressful day. Before retiring, I went outside to check on Snoopy's situation. There was no change. I covered him with a cotton sheet and said, "Goodnight, see you in the morning." He moved his eyes. I think he was trying to say, "Goodbye."

Through the night, I could hear the back screen door bang at regular intervals. It was Kevin going outside to check on Snoopy. I awoke unusually early the next morning. I could hear the murder of crows conducting their regular morning meeting in the large gum tree several houses down the road, but this did not usually wake me. I was used to that noise each morning.

I put on my dressing gown and went downstairs to see Snoopy. In my mind, I was planning what to feed him now that he should be well. I arrived at the spot where he was lying the night before. He was not there. My heart jumped with joy.

Then I looked to my left. He was lying approximately two metres away from where he'd been the night before. He was dead to our world. I cannot describe the sadness I felt in that moment. It was much worse than when Elle passed away. We all knew Elle did not have long to live because of her recurring cancer. This death was totally unexpected. It came without warning, so I had a lot of trouble managing the ensuing sadness that blanketed me.

I sat at the bottom step of the stairs leading to the upper level and just looked at him. I did not cry. The lack of tears disappointed me. It was inside me, but I couldn't release the grief, at least not just yet. I wondered why Snoopy had moved two metres to the left of where he was lying the night before. I surmised that he might have been uncomfortably warm. It was a warm night. He must have summoned what strength he had left and moved himself to find the slight breeze that regularly wafted down the side of our house most nights. That is where he expired. I placed the white cotton sheet over him.

I had to let Anne know this very sad news. She must have been awake wondering if Snoopy had made it through the night.

I walked into our bedroom and said, "He's gone. He must have slipped away sometime during the night."

Anne's reaction mirrored mine.

"I don't want him cremated like Zowie was. He needs to be with Elle," I said. Anne could do nothing but agree. "I'm gonna' see where I can bury him, then I'll get us a coffee." Again Anne agreed.

As I was making my way to the kitchen, Kevin arrived from downstairs. Tears were in free-flow, streaming down his cheeks. His tear drops were like heavy raindrops on a window pane. Silently I wished I could get rid of my grief just like that. My grief is still with me to this day, and it doesn't seem to want to go away.

Kevin looked at me with bloodshot eyes and announced, "Me best mate's gone. He went about five this mornin'."

He couldn't stand up any longer being so overcome with grief. He sat at the kitchen table looking at the floor. I wondered if he was imagining Snoopy lying there, as Snoopy often did when he was ready for breakfast.

Kevin looked up at me with such a sad face and said, "I did everythin' I could for 'im."

This was one of those difficult moments in life when you can quickly damage a relationship by choosing to say words you don't really mean. I was feeling so angry and sad at the same time. I chose to console Kevin with, "We know you did, Kevie. Don't blame yourself. We're not blaming you for this."

I stayed in the kitchen with Kevin for a while, and then I decided to make coffee for us all.

#

Much later that same morning, after composing ourselves, we were sitting on the front verandah, going through the motions of sipping more coffee and exchanging views about Snoopy's demise, when I abruptly changed the course of our conversation by stating, "I'll bury Snoopy in the new raised garden bed I built before we went away—that way he can still contribute to this household by raising the vegetables." I was trying to make light of this very sad occasion. My aim was to lift our spirits, to have a bit of chuckle because I don't like being sad all the time. My strategy didn't work.

"No you won't!" objected Anne. "He needs to be with Elle. Let's go around the back yard and find a good spot for him—he needs to be near Elle." I agreed.

So we walked our back yard. Anne pointed to a spot off the concrete pathway. It happened to be the hardest ground to dig in a confined space, but I agreed it was the best place for him because, on the other side of the pathway, lay his adoptive mother, Elle.

Kevin said he would give me a hand, but he couldn't do much except hand me the digging tools given the limitations caused by his disability.

I started digging around nine o'clock and finished the digging just before noon. I went to where Snoopy was lying and adjusted the white cotton sheet fully around him so I could lift him. I did not cover his face. I took several photographs of the big fella using my iPhone, and then placed him, gently as I could, into his final resting place. I needed the photographs of him to remember him. I am a terribly visual person.

We gathered at his grave and looked at him for the final time. I then covered his face with the white cotton sheet, and said a few words like, "We're going to miss you terribly around here, big fella! Say gidday to Elle and tell her we miss her too," then I returned the soil back from whence it came. At times, when I feel sad, I will look at the photographs of Snoopy on my phone. It helps me to focus my grief and to slowly heal up that big hole left in my heart.

#

Several weeks went by after Snoopy's passing. Anne and I were back into our usual routine of avoiding Kevin in the mornings and catching up with him on our verandah during the afternoons. The first few weeks of our collective afternoon chats were all about Snoopy. Those chats helped to fill the void left behind by his passing. We were continuing to manage our grief.

One Sunday afternoon, Kevin did not return home at his usual time. Anne and I took that opportunity to have a heart-to-heart chat concerning Kevin.

"Maybe he's had enough of staying with us and has gone home?" Anne theorised.

"No, he would've told us,"

"He's got to go. I feel very uncomfortable having him here."

Kevin returned home after dark that day. As he came through our front gate displaying his usual access difficulties, I blurted out, "Did you go to the church today?"

"Why do ya wanna know?"

"It's late. Being Sunday, I thought you might have gone to church, or Sunday School, or something like that."

"I'll be right up as long as you have a coldie there for me!"

Kevin ascended our internal stairs and positioned himself into his usual chair. He explained that he had been delayed by some old friends he met unexpectedly at the bowls club. We then enjoyed several drinks over little conversation. Kevin exclaimed after he had partaken of his last gulp of amber liquid, "I need to have me puff."

We went inside and left Kevin to his medication. Anne said she was not feeling well and went to lie down as she whispered to me, "Now is a good opportunity for you to let Kevin know he needs to move on."

I nodded. I went into the kitchen to start preparing our evening meal. As I was role-playing in my head about what I was going to say to my uncle, the verandah door swung open, then with a bang, Kevin stomped into the room with his legs stepping high.

"Youse know how I feel 'bout religion — no place in modern society — it was needed in the old days to control the chaos. Today we have order in the form of government, be it capitalism, socialism, or communism—the one closest to religion is communism."

"How do you figure that?"

"Well communism comes from the word *communion*—you'd know all about that havin' bin an old altar boy."

Without any further challenges from me, Kevin then went on to lecture to me his version of the biblical world as he stood awkwardly in the kitchen.

According to Pastor Kevin, there have been three stages of *enlightenment*: The Old Testament, The New Testament, and then the passing of the baton from the *diplomat* to the prodigal son.

"Diplomat?"

"Yeah, Christ worked in the diplomatic service."

Kevin explained that the Old Testament, "is about creation, much the same as recalled by our first nations peoples—Baiame's hand—the Hebrew and the Christian God was a proud creator but a vengeful Lord," lectured Kevin from his pulpit. "He gave his creation autonomy but didn't like it when his pride and joy didn't follow his road map."

"Road map?"

"His master plan for us," replied Pastor Kevin. "We, youse, me and everyone on this planet are collectively His creation doin' bad things in the early days — He didn't like it — so He sent plagues, pestilence, fire and flood... one vengeful rage after another finally saw us almost wiped out by a big flood—except He called in selected species two by two, into that floatin' zoo to keep His creation goin'."

"Go on."

"Then comes the New Testament: it records a lotta remorse experienced by the big fella; in short, He decided to send a diplomat to fix things up between us. Christ arrived to show us how ta talk to Him, how ta respect Him, and how ta live our given lives without His need to interfere."

"An interesting view of the Bible but what about the Prodigal son? Where does he fit in?"

"Christ was the diplomat—we are *collectively* the Prodigal Son. We're tasked with making our way back to where it all started: Paradise!"

"I feel much better after that sermon — thanks — I'll sleep well tonight."

I decided this was not the right time to have *that* conversation. Anne joined us for dinner. It was a non-event. The food was not well prepared and there was little conversation. After the evening news was delivered via the *idiot box*, Kevin bade us, "good night", and then departed to his room.

#

Kevin and I sat on our front verandah. It was mid-morning Monday. I decided to have a chat with him about his future with Anne and me while he was in his Mr Hyde state.

This was initially a big mistake.

"So Kevie, how are you feeling now that you've stayed with us so much this year? Are you over your demons?" I enquired.

There was a pause in the conversation. Kevin looked around and then to the east, as if seeking divine inspiration, as he would often do when he was thinking about things on his mind.

"I'm in a good frame of mind thanks to youse. The union trained me how to do that," he quietly replied.

"One reason why I wanted to have this chat with you, Kevie, is about Anne," I said. "You have verbally abused her three times now without cause, and each time it has occurred in the morning. I can't have you upsetting Anne all the time. Once you do, her anxiety level goes right up, and it takes weeks to come back down to normal. I can't have you staying with us any more," I stated sternly.

Kevin again looked east and said with a raised voice, "I've been thinkin' about hittin' the road agin. I can pack up and leave in the mornin'."

"We're not in a rush to get you to leave. No worries for you to stay until the grand final is over in about two weeks' time. Then why don't you go back home and patch it up with Steven?" I counselled.

"I don't have a son, so no patchin' up needed," was his grumpy reply.

"You can't deny you have family—your son!" I interjected, to which Kevin said, "No son would kick his father out no matter what the problem was!"

I again counselled, "I'm sure Steven is regretting what he did, and would probably welcome you home. Give him a call before you get there, like when you arrive here."

A much angrier Kevin replied, "I don't have a son!"

There was much venom in his voice.

I backed off to let *sleeping dogs lie*.

I stood up and went into the kitchen to let him cool down. I returned with glasses and two pre-mix bottles of

Kevin's favourite drink: rum and Coke. His eyes lit up when he saw the glasses, but then said, "A bit early, isn't it?"

He was looking at me for approval, so I replied, "There's a pub open somewhere in the world! And anyhow, this is good medicine!" I then handed him a full glass of rum and Coke (usually he would only take a half-glass). So we again saluted the memory of Snoopy and then drank several bottles of the pre-mix drink.

Kevin was now feeling relaxed. Mr Hyde was departing. Glimpses of Dr Jekyll came shining through.

"I do very much appreciate what youse have done for me after Steven kicked me out. I arrived here not knowin' what I was gunna' do or where I was gunna' go. I was thinkin' about doin' away with meself. You and Anne have restored the faith an' belief I had in meself. I feel like I can hit the road now an' do the best I can for others I meet."

"Good on you, Kevie," I coached. "Maybe you can go find your old mate Satts and have a bloody good time catching up with him?" I encouraged.

Kevin replied enthusiastically, "Good idea!"

Knowing that Kevin was now in his afternoon mood, I said, "And for Christ's sake, go patch it up with Stevie!"

Kevin thought about that in his usual way, then said, "I think I will. I'll go back and see if I can find out why he kicked me out. He never told me his reason, just gave me an eviction notice. Maybe we can patch things up, but I'll go north first to see if I can find Satts. Thanks."

#

The football grand final came and went, and so Kevin prepared himself to go on the road again.

"Goodbye, Snoop Dog," he said as he stood over Snoopy's grave, a tear or two appearing.

We both walked to his white van, where he had assembled his belongings on the footpath under the golden melaleuca tree, the exact location when he first arrived.

I assisted him to again adjust his mattress so it "won't dig me in the ribs". We loaded up his large tank of water and his luggage. We checked his brake lights and signal lights for proper function. He was ready to go.

As we finished loading, we stepped back off the kerb and Kevin then hugged me and said a simple, "Thanks." We shook hands.

Anne then yelled from our verandah, "Look after yourself, Kevie. Safe driving!"

Kevin looked up at her and returned, "You look after yerself too, beautiful lady—thanks!"

I stood there at the kerb watching the white van disappear around our street corner. I waved as it turned. I could not see Kevin behind the steering wheel due to the light reflection on the van's side window, but I am sure he would have seen me waving. I then returned to sit with Anne on the verandah. I looked around. It had been some twelve months since we first had the verandah constructed. It was now shabby from constant use. It needed a coat of paint.

We both watched the blazing late spring sun rise above the golden melaleuca tree as we shared several black coffees and a conversation about Kevie.

"I wonder where he will end up?" Anne enquired of the universe as she looked east, the same way Kevin did when he was trying to figure things out. Then she suddenly said, "If he wants to come back here, don't invite him. I don't want him here!"

I answered Anne on behalf of the universe, "I'm hoping he goes straight home to see Steven—to patch things up so he's got a place to live. But you know Kevin—he'll come to a fork in the road and suddenly life becomes a big adventure for him once again!"

After Kevin departed, Anne's anxiety level returned to normal. It was pleasing for me to see her at times spontaneously laughing about nothing. It was a good feeling to have our house back to normal. Several weeks after Kevin's departure came an evening phone call, right on six o'clock.

Scammer time, I thought to myself as I lifted the receiver and said, "Hello. State police, fraud squad."

The voice at the other end of the line asked, "How's Anne?"

It was Kevin.

"She's all right — good as gold," I said, then remembered this might be him angling for an encore. Recalling Anne's orders, I added, "I'm always now the optimist, you know—you taught me that. She still struggles each day. She had a bad night's sleep last night, so she's catching up with sleep as we speak. It took a long time for her to settle down today."

"Give her my love."

I guessed that he was inside his van and had just had his *smoke*. "Where are you?"

"Ballina."

"Stay away from those women and their crazy dogs!"

"I'll give youse a call in few weeks," he said, then hung up his end of the line.

When I think back and analyse this very short verbal exchange, I have come to the conclusion that Kevin was in our neighbourhood and was fishing to see how Anne's condition was before asking to come back. When I told him she was still having problems, I think he finally decided to move on.

Where Kevin has moved on to, we don't know, because he hasn't called us since. I can only assume he never went travelling north looking for Satts, nor was he in Ballina.

Two days after Kevin's last call came another call, right on six o'clock.

"Scammers or Kevin?" I mumbled to myself as I lifted the handset, then stated in an authoritative voice, "Hello. You have reached the federal police."

"Hi, bro'. It's your big brother Terry. I've got some very sad news for you. Stevie, Kevin's son, passed away yesterday afternoon."

Chapter 13
Reflections

We found out several weeks after that fateful telephone call from my brother Terry that Steven had been having lung trouble for several years. He lost the use of his right lung twelve months before he took his final breath. We understand Steven collapsed and died one afternoon on his way home from work.

We don't know if Kevie ever made it back home in time to patch things up with Steven, nor could we confirm whether he attended the funeral. We think not in each case, but we live in hope that he did.

#

My paternal uncle Kevin came to visit unexpectedly one summer. We didn't know he was concealing emotional pain. Kevin only wanted to stay with us for a short while, but he stayed with us for a long while. During his tenancy, we found out what that emotional pain was that upset him so. The pain had troubled him so much that he finally could not keep it concealed any longer. Kevin revealed to us that he had been evicted by his beloved son from his son's property. Prior to his eviction, Kevin had handed over his very successful business to his son, Steven. Apart from being very proud of his son, this act of kindness toward his son made the eviction hurt even more.

Kevin is a proud man. He is self-made. The eviction was something Kevin never saw coming, nor could he process or handle it. He held much empathy for former Prime Minister Gough Whitlam, after this happening in his life because they both suffered from a very hurtful *eviction*. Each eviction caused Kevin great anxiety and depression, resulting in a couple of very low points in his life. After suffering this personal eviction, and then not knowing which way to turn, he was thinking of doing away with himself. As if on autopilot, he arrived unexpectedly at our home.

We are often reminded that there are two sides to every argument. We know my uncle's side of the story, but we don't know Steven's side—and now we never will.

Anne and I had gleaned from his tenancy with us that Kevin was not the man he used to be. The cheery, happy-go-lucky character, my uncle's trademark throughout his life, was still around each afternoon, but his personality seemed to have split into two halves. Each morning we battled to entertain *Mr Hyde*; each afternoon we were entertained by *Dr Jekyll*.

I always suspected smoking had a lot to do with those "Mr Hyde" episodes. I was a smoker in my late teens and early twenties, until I realised smoking didn't suit my personality. The marijuana I smoked back then caused me to giggle incessantly. It then led me into long-term melancholy states. Getting up out of that deep pit was my biggest battle.

I remember lying in bed one day, just staring at myself in the mirror, much the same as the doped-up surfboard riders do when they go *out back*, beyond the breaking waves to simply sit on their surfboard, and stare and ponder for hours. I remember thinking to myself that day, *Geez you're ugly!* Obviously back then I had a very low opinion of myself. Perhaps this same melancholy problem has crept into my uncle's mornings.

Today I have a very good opinion of myself, maybe because of some recent subliminal help from my paternal uncle.

Kevin has gone through much suffering in his life, but those "chapters", as he refers to them, "are challenges". He would often say, sometimes ad nauseam, "There are three cardinal times in ya life: ya born; ya live; and ya die. Youse have no control over the first and last, but ya sure have choices in between."

His enthusiasm for living has not been dented by loves lost, death, being illiterate in his early years, medical challenges, nor his personal suffering because of his eviction. Those challenges through his life have only slowed him down.

My uncle has faced off all his demons, and he has won each battle. He has passed through life's gauntlet still the lovable larrikin standing today.

My summation of my uncle is that he is basically an introvert living as an extrovert in an ever-changing scary world. Look around you. Pick up this morning's newspaper and read it. Look at the evening news on television tonight. Most of the reporting is to do with the awful part of living. We can be scared by it all, or we can accept what we cannot change it, and so not let it affect us. My uncle has done just that.

During his first coming, I felt that my uncle had given me something, but I wasn't quite sure what it was. During his second coming, I finally realised what he had given me: he had taught me how to be an optimist, and he had taught me the art of stimulating conversation.

Everyone knows of, or needs, a Kevie in their lives. If you are down, Kevie will be there to pick you up. If you don't know which way to turn, Kevie will tell you to head for a fork in the road and then take any turn, left or right, because each turn in your life is a waiting adventure. And sometimes when you are feeling sorry for yourself, then just think of Kevie's smiling outlook, his skinny legs, and his happy disposition regardless of his constant battles with his physical limitations.

One thing for certain is that Kevie is out there somewhere, travelling around this big country of ours. The only decision we think he would be making these days is, "Do I turn left, or do I turn right?" after reaching each proverbial fork along the road of life.

I remember reading an unforgettable ancient First Nations Proverb a long time ago. It stated, *we are all visitors to this time, this place. We are just passing through. Our purpose is to observe, to grow, to love... and then we return home.* Without knowing it, I think Kevin is living this ancient proverb.

We don't know where Kevie is, nor what he is doing right now, but we are sure he is living his life to the fullest, as best he can, making people around him feel good, and enjoying the best chicken schnitzel he has ever tasted, as he tells each and every one he encounters in his travels: "Be the best you can be with what you've got."